CONTENTS

INTRODUCTION

The National Curriculum
Understanding Shakespeare
Appreciating Shakespeare

William Shakespeare has not been dubbed 'the greatest English poet' for nothing. Shakespeare is a vital part of the English National Curriculum; during your years at school you are expected to study two of his plays in detail.

You have probably come across some of Shakespeare's work before, particularly if you have done your English SATs. You might have been introduced to short sections of his plays when you were quite young, possibly even at primary school. This is probably because English teachers like Shakespeare, and generally enjoy teaching it!

DID YOU KNOW?
The title of the television programme *The Darling Buds of May* is in fact a line from a Shakespearean sonnet?

Even if you think you know nothing about Shakespeare, you are probably more familiar with his words than you are aware:

- How many of you already knew that 'Romeo, Romeo, wherefore art thou Romeo?' comes from *Romeo and Juliet*?

- Or that 'Friends, Romans, countrymen, lend me your ears,' is from *Julius Caesar*?

- Or what about some of those phrases you have been hearing for years, such as when your mum tells you she is 'at her wit's end' with you, or that your ability to get five GCSEs is 'a foregone conclusion'?

Shakespeare crops up all the time, wherever language and words are used to convey meaning. It is a vital part of our culture and the history of English literature.

THINK ABOUT IT

How many of these phrases do you know? Look where they come from!

The course of true love never did run smooth *A Midsummer Night's Dream*
That was laid on with a trowel *As You Like It*
And thereby hangs a tale *The Taming of the Shrew*
The game is up *Cymbeline*
Method in my madness *Hamlet*
To play the fool *Hamlet*
Every dog has its day *Hamlet*
Wear my heart on my sleeve *Othello*
Jealousy ... is the green-eyed monster *Othello*

This book is intended to give you some basic information about some of the more well known of Shakespeare's thirty-seven plays, along with a 'tool kit' for understanding and appreciation.

We hope you find it useful and that you enjoy your Shakespeare!

CATEGORISING THE PLAYS

Histories and tragedies
Comedies and romances
Problem plays

William Shakespeare (1564-1616) wrote thirty-seven plays altogether; no mean feat for someone who died when he was in his mid-fifties. The plays can be separated into different groups or categories depending on their subject-matter, tone and theme.

However, this is easier said than done, and critics have argued over these categorisations for many years. Most people now accept the following broad groupings:

- The histories

- The tragedies

- The comedies

- The romances

- We also have a 'cop-out' grouping called the 'problem' plays!

Shakespeare used the conventions of play-writing which came from ancient Greece, and in particular the great thinker, Aristotle. Aristotle identified and categorised many of these elements which have now come to be accepted parts of play-writing convention and form. Shakespeare's tragedies and comedies all have adapted classical or Aristotelian elements in them.

The histories

These are the plays which deal with a definite event or series of events in English history, and take as their title the king of England central to each story. Shakespeare chose to chronicle the monarchies spanning two centuries, from the late fifteenth century to the mid-sixteenth century. This was a period of turmoil, political unrest and civil war in Britain, which was calmed only when Henry VII married the House of York heiress, Elizabeth, to bring together the two warring sides of Lancaster and York.

DID YOU KNOW?
The history plays are based on fact, or facts as Shakespeare would have known them at the time of writing. The events he chronicles are basically correct, although he was far more concerned with personality than the political.

The plays which span this time are;

- *King John*
- *Richard II*
- *Richard III*
- *Henry IV* (parts 1 and 2)
- *Henry V*
- *Henry VI* (parts 1, 2 and 3)
- *Henry VIII*

Shakespeare stuck closely to historical sources for these plays, exploring and analysing the nature and responsibility of kingship.

The tragedies

The basic definition of a Shakespearean tragedy is that the central character falls from a position of greatness owing to a 'fatal flaw' in their nature. People die and it all ends terribly. The audience is meant to leave the theatre with a strong sense of regret, or 'if only'! The great tragedies are:

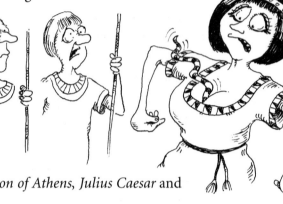

– *Macbeth*

– *Othello*

– *King Lear*

– *Hamlet*

– *Antony and Cleopatra*

Some people also include *Timon of Athens*, *Julius Caesar* and *Coriolanus* in this category.

DID YOU KNOW?

Remember the famous discussion of the meaning of the term 'tragedy' in the play *Educating Rita* by Willie Russell:

FRANK: *The sort of thing you read in the paper that's reported as being tragic, 'Man Killed By Falling Tree', is not a tragedy.*

RITA: *It is for the poor sod under the tree.*

Frank is trying to explain the difference between life tragedy and dramatic tragedy; the central character of a dramatic tragedy has to take pre-ordained, inevitable steps towards his (and it is always his) own downfall, and ignores all the warnings along the way.

The comedies

Shakespeare followed classical traditions ▶ see pp 14-25 in the structure of the comedies. They all contain some idea of mistaken identity. Disguise is a common device, particularly women dressing as men to liberate themselves from the shackles which society imposed upon them.

Escape was another familar idea, particularly the idea of escape from the town into the countryside.

Love is always the main theme and all the comedies have to end happily, of course, with a marriage. All mistakes are sorted out and lovers correctly paired off. There is also a 'baddie' who poses some kind of threat, but he will be defeated and unhappy by the end of the play. These plays include:

- *A Midsummer Night's Dream*
- *The Comedy of Errors*
- *Twelfth Night*
- *Much Ado About Nothing*
- *As You Like It*
- *Love's Labours Lost*
- *The Merry Wives of Windsor*

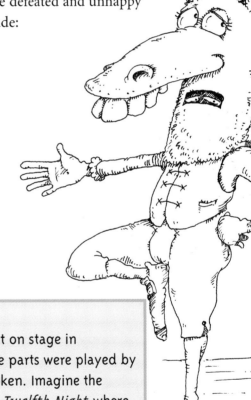

DID YOU KNOW?
Women were not allowed to act on stage in Elizabethan times, so all female parts were played by boys whose voices had not broken. Imagine the confusion in a comedy such as *Twelfth Night* where the female part, played by a boy, had to pretend to be male!

The romances

The Romances often explore the relationship between parent and child. Written later in Shakespeare's life, they are more serious in tone than the comedies, although all tend to have a comfortable, if not 'happy' conclusion. These plays are:

- *Cymbeline*

- *A Winter's Tale*

- *Pericles*

- *The Tempest*

The romances deal with human relationships. Although the plot lines are far from 'real' in a believable sense (in *A Winter's Tale*, Leontes is cruel to his wife so she feigns her own death and pretends she is a statue of herself; hubbie falls for this completely) the emotions and human behaviour are totally real. Jealousy, revenge, power and regret are main themes.

DID YOU KNOW?
The term 'romance' does not mean 'romantic' in the sense of romantic love. *The Oxford English Dictionary* defines the term romance to mean 'any narrative work dealing with events and characters remote from ordinary life'.

The 'problem' plays

There is another group; the tragicomedies, dark comedies or 'problem' plays (plays that are a problem to categorise!) These have a strong romantic theme, and contain more than one element of tragedy and comedy. This group includes:

- *The Merchant of Venice*

- *Measure for Measure*

- *All's Well That Ends Well*

- *The Taming of the Shrew*

- *Romeo and Juliet*

DID YOU KNOW?

The Merchant of Venice was originally called *The Tragedy of Shylock the Jew*, which gives us some indication of how Shakespeare wanted his character to be viewed by the audience.

You might be saying to yourself at this stage, 'if categorising the plays causes all this confusion, why do we need to do it at all?' The answer relates to the earlier point about classical Greek Theatre. Shakespeare wrote within an expected, agreed and recognisable framework of conventions. His audience expected certain conventions from a comedy, a tragedy, etc., and therefore he had to provide these. If he had ended a tragedy with the hero walking off into the sunset with a beautiful woman on his arm there would have been an outcry!

N
O
T
E
S

HIGHER PERFORMANCE

Tudor and Stuart England was a period of political turmoil. Henry VIII had turned his back on the only order the people had ever known: the Catholic Church. He had been excommunicated for divorcing his first wife, Catherine of Aragon in order to marry Anne Boleyn. England was divided between loyalty to the Pope and the Church of Rome, and loyalty to the Crown and the new Protestant Church of England. When Henry VIII died, his daughter Mary Tudor became queen and England reverted to Catholicism; when Elizabeth I became queen in 1558 she reinstated Protestantism, which caused tremendous battles with the Catholics who thought that Mary, Queen of Scots should be the rightful (Catholic) ruler of England.

We see echoes of this unrest in the tremendous political turmoil in Northern Ireland, similarly brought about by division between Catholic and Protestant loyalty. It is also vital to remember that in the sixteenth century, religion was the only source of stability and order in a world which knew nothing about physical, chemical or biological science. Religion gave the answers everyone sought: why we are here, who created us, what happened when we died, etc. Without religion nothing made sense. Elizabethans still believed that the world was flat; America was only discovered mid-way through the century; the crowned ruler was second only to God, and atheism was not a concept at all.

Theatre mirrored this need to give order and security, which is why dramatic convention was so much a part of every dramatist's work. William Shakespeare's genius rests partly in his ability to address this idea of convention; to manipulate and question the previously unquestionable.

What light does the study of Shakespeare shed on modern political problems?

Quiz

1. How many plays did William Shakespeare write?

2. Name the five different categories or types of play.

macbeth, Twelve nights King Henry Caesar

3. Were the history plays based upon fact or fiction?

King Henry II

4. Name the Greek thinker and playwright who influenced Shakespearean structure and plot.

5. What kind of character is the central figure in a tragedy?

6. What was the 'problem' with the problem plays?

7. What would cause great confusion in casting a comedy?

8. Name two famous comedies.

9. Name two famous tragedies.

10. Name two famous history plays.

Answers

1. 37.
2. History, tragedy, comedy, romance, problem.
3. Fact.
4. Aristotle.
5. The tragic hero.
6. Difficult to categorise.
7. When the plot called for the female character to disguise herself as a boy, given that female parts were played by boys in the first place!
8. Look it up – see page 9.
9. Look it up – see page 8.
10. Look it up – see page 7.

SHAKESPEARE'S THEATRE

Classical traditions

Aristotelian unities

Elizabethan theatre

Before we start on a detailed examination of the structure of each play, here are some basic ideas about Elizabethan drama which Shakespeare had.

Classical traditions

During the fifteenth century, English culture went through a period which has come to be known as 'The Renaissance':

✳ Renaissance means 'rebirth'; a reawakening of interest in classical literature, art, music and poetry.

✳ Ancient Greek poets, scholars and philosophers were studied in detail.

✳ French and Italian writers and painters became very popular.

✳ Greek plays were performed for audiences across the land.

✳ The theatre became part of the world of ordinary people, rather than kept for the aristocracy and nobility.

We have all grown up on a diet of television and multimedia. Elizabethans, most of whom were illiterate, were weaned on oral story-telling and plays. They reacted in much the same way that a modern audience responds to a pantomime performance.

THOU ART ROPEY

BOO

GERROFF

Shakespeare was writing his plays for an audience who would physically come to see them. He was not writing for some student who would sit in a dusty classroom four hundred years later and agonise over Friar Lawrence's motivation for his involvement in Romeo and Juliet's romance, or whether Macbeth was a monster or a hen-pecked husband! He was writing to entertain a large group of people who had all paid their penny to stand in an uncomfortable theatre and be taken away from the harsh reality of their lives for a few hours.

The Elizabethan audience had certain expectations. They knew what a comedy was and what a tragedy was. They expected a comedy to end with at least one marriage. They assumed that a tragedy would end with the death of the central character along with probably lots of other people!

Therefore, Shakespeare was working within a certain expected framework, largely modelled on classical Greek theatre. This gave him two things:

– Conventions within which he could structure his play

– A starting point from which he could develop his ideas

This kind of assumed knowledge works in exactly the same way with modern soap-operas; we assume that there will be certain 'stock' characters within each one, such as the villain, the comic ne'er-do-well or rogue, the love-interest or 'romantic lead', the wise older resident who has seen it all, etc. We also expect a certain time-length from each episode, and a cliffhanger ending.

THINK ABOUT IT

How shocked would we be if suddenly *EastEnders* finished one Thursday evening with a song and dance routine? Or if everyone in *Coronation Street* was suddenly killed off in a freak air disaster and the series was announced over for ever?

We know how our soap operas are supposed to work; we all share knowledge of that framework or 'genre' in the same way that Shakespeare and his audience shared their knowledge of tragedy, comedy and romance. The ancient Greeks loved the theatre, and most modern drama is modelled around the rules they invented for genre, structure and plot.

Aristotelian unities

Writers of classical Greek drama, particularly Aristotle, established rules about the way theatre should be constructed, the dramatic unities of time, place and action.

Unity of time

The length of time taken by the action in a play should be around the same as the time taken to perform it. The writer was allowed to extend the period of imaginary action to twenty-four hours. Even Shakespeare with all his genius found this a very cumbersome convention and only really adheres to it in *The Tempest*, which has a time span of around four hours. The only other play that has a short duration of time is *Romeo and Juliet*, where the action takes place over five days.

Unity of place

The scene should be the same one throughout the play. Maybe Shakespeare felt that this would be a little dull for his audience. Whatever the reason, it is only in *The Tempest* where 'an uninhabited island' is the single setting direction.

Unity of action

The play should have one main plot and any other plots must be subordinate to that. This is one unity that Shakespeare does maintain throughout most of his work.

What is remarkable about the way Shakespeare subordinated plots and characters is that they will at some stage have something to do with the main plot; look at Lorenzo and Jessica's discussion of the intransigent nature of love in Act V of The Merchant of Venice; they make some interesting observations as they prepare to greet the two pairs of newlyweds Portia and Bassanio and Gratiano and Nerissa. Or what about the Porter in *Macbeth*, who delivers a whole speech describing the nature of the inhabitants of Hell, claiming that all are 'equivocators' or treacherous liars? Could it be his master he is inadvertently referring to?

The idea of a drama

The basic concept overriding all others in any play is the idea of conflict and resolution. There must be some problem or conflict which is sorted out by the end of the story. The problem may be between two individuals, or two nations, or within one person as in *Macbeth*, where his private conflict of interest becomes one of national importance to Scotland, and eventually to England. A more detailed examination of this idea will follow in the section Key Plays – Macbeth ▶ see pp 84–90.

A drama is usually a narrative, which means it is telling a story. Drama is all about tension; dramatic tension caused by the interplay of human relationships mainly. In fact, it could be said that the main definition of a play is a narrative which explores the tension created by human behaviour.

THINK ABOUT IT

When you read a Shakespeare play, try to visualise it being performed. Drama only comes alive in the hands of actors who make their own interpretations of the dialogue and actions. By a small gesture or intonation, an actor may make Shakespeare's words stunningly relevant to current events. This insight will not necessarily reveal itself just by reading the play. Reading plays, without trying to imagine them being performed, can distort them.

NOTES

Mechanics of the Elizabethan theatre

We are a sophisticated audience these days. We think nothing of going to see a film that has cost millions of pounds to make. We consume hours of television every day, and have extremely sophisticated theatres. We take for granted such things as elaborate special effects, stage sets, lighting rigs, sound effects, music, costume and stage properties. All these techniques contribute greatly to the visual and emotional experience of watching a piece of drama.

However, none of these things was available to the Elizabethan theatre company:

– They had a wooden stage with a curtain.

– Costumes were in limited supply.

– Theatres were open to the elements.

– Plays had to be shown in daylight, and in good weather!

– Actors came on with 'torches' or candles to signify darkness.

– Characters were often given lines which announced to the audience where the scene was supposed to be.

The Chorus

This is another idea from classical theatre which Shakespeare made great use of, particularly in *Henry V* and *Romeo and Juliet*. **The Chorus was an actor, part of the company, who would give the audience some extra information, possibly contextualising or explaining the action for them.** The Chorus in *Henry V* is particularly interesting to study in terms of the requirement that the audience suspend belief; the limitations of the theatre are directly apologised for:

> *But pardon, gentles all,*
> *The flat unraised spirits that hath dar'd*
> *On this unworthy scaffold to bring forth*
> *So great an object: can this cockpit hold*
> *The vasty fields of France? or may we cram*
> *Within this wooden O the very casques*
> *That did affright the air at Agincourt?*

Generally the Chorus introduced the action and summarised it periodically, presumably to ensure everyone was keeping up with the plot! The audience were totally familiar with the concept of the Chorus. Although we would be very surprised if someone popped up at the start of *Inspector Morse* and had a chat directly to camera, the Elizabethans, who were consummate theatre-goers, expected their Chorus.

Given the limitations of the Elizabethan theatre, the Chorus provided vital support to the action. They could fill the gaps, add detail to events which had apparently occurred before the beginning, or between Acts, and so on. They could bridge gaps in time, point out matters of interest and generally assist the structure of the play.

NOTES

Other elements

Boys will be girls

Acting was seen as unfeminine and disreputable, 'not a job for a lady'. So all female roles in the plays had to be performed by young boys dressed as women. Imagine the confusion when it came to a comedy, where one of the expectations was that there would be some kind of disguise set-up, usually a female character dressing up as a boy! In fact, Shakespeare deliberately used this rule by developing situations, particularly in the comedies, where the girl character had to disguise herself as a boy, thus making the boy actor more convincing. It is one reason why William Shakespeare wrote so few great female parts. The boy actors were called 'apprentices' and were often in great demand; until their voices broke and they began to grow facial hair, that is! These apprentices were extremely good actors; they had to be, considering the demands of the female roles that Shakespeare wrote. So the next time you think about Lady Macbeth, remember that her part would have originally been played by a boy of twelve. Amazing, isn't it?

Jobs for the boys

Shakespeare always had someone in mind for the part as he was writing it. Some argue that this is the reason the strong character of Falstaff is 'killed off' in *Henry V*, when he was such a strong presence in the *Henry IV* plays. Possibly the actor who played him was unavailable. There is a far more juicy explanation for the 'killing off' of Falstaff however; his character was apparently loosely based upon a nobleman whose family, the Brookes, were enraged by the perceived mockery of their relative. Shakespeare could have bowed under the weight of powerful pressure. The female parts were conceived in the same way. It needed a very good actor to carry off the roles of Lady Macbeth and Cleopatra.

Always a good laugh

There is always a comic character, even in *Macbeth* (the Porter) and *King Lear* (the Fool). With two or three hours of 'high drama' the audience needed a break from the dramatic tension. In *Romeo and Juliet*, this comes with the servants getting ready for Juliet's marriage to Paris. In *Macbeth*, the Porter's speech comes just after the murder of Duncan. It was a bit of a rest for the nerves after all that tension. ▶ see p 90

These comic characters and interludes nearly always had something interesting and relevant to do with the main plot, and would appear to be commenting on what was going on without being in any way involved. The Porter's speech in *Macbeth* is all about 'equivocation' or lying and being deceitful. He describes his job as being 'Porter of Hell-Gate' and comments on the world being full of evil.

Shakespeare mixes comic and other effects, as, for example at the end of *Antony and Cleopatra* when a clown brings in the snakes with which Cleopatra will commit suicide. This is the last moment one would expect a playwright to make his audience laugh, just prior to the tragic climax of the whole play, yet the scene works magnificently. The audience relaxes so that they respond to the climax with even more concentration and attention than would otherwise have been the case.

Talking to yourself

The soliloquy can sometimes confuse a reader of a Shakespeare play. The audience knew that when a central character was delivering one of these he or she was merely thinking aloud. There was no other way of letting the audience know the inner workings of a character's mind than by making an 'aside'. The content of a soliloquy is always honest, and contains vitally important thoughts. It is a dramatic device used to give the audience information or to reveal motives and intentions that are not revealed to other characters.

And finally...

when you are struggling to come up with an original idea for your creative writing coursework, it is worth bearing in mind that Shakespeare, arguably the best writer in the world, never used an original storyline in his plays! His history plays were all based on fact, and all the other stories come from much older Italian and French tales which he adapted and developed for the stage. We can forgive him for this though, since he did as a result, manage to come up with some of the best plays the world has ever known! Obviously he didn't just copy the stories; he developed and altered the original source material to come up with a fascinating new work every time.

NOTES

HIGHER PERFORMANCE

The essence of William Shakespeare's writing rests in his ability to take stock 'formats' such as comedy and tragedy; stock character 'types' such as hero, villain, heroine, and manipulate their behaviour to add depth to the experience for the audience. Shakespeare is studied now in as much intensity purely because of this inherent depth. Macbeth is a good example of a tragic hero whom we despise on one level for his cruelty and lust for power; however it is impossible to sum him up as a 'villain' motivated purely by power and greed. It is likewise impossible to look at the way Shakespeare constructed his plots with one simple overview. Take for example the end of *The Merchant of Venice*, where the villain Shylock has been defeated and the romantic pairings have been concluded satisfactorily. There is, however, a sense of unease that all is not as it should be.

Ask yourself how Shakespeare creates characters who have vices and virtues in their make-up.

Is this why they offer such interesting challenges to actors?

Does each generation re-interpret Shakespeare for itself?

Quiz

1. What does 'Renaissance' mean?

2. What is another word for 'genre'?

3. Name the three classical unities.

4. What is the basic need and function of drama?

5. Give one reason why language played such a huge part in Elizabethan theatre.

6. What was the function of the chorus?

7. Give one reason for the use of comic characters in serious plays.

8. What is a soliloquy?

9. Name two comic characters from the plays we have discussed.

10. Where did William Shakespeare get most of the inspiration for his plot lines?

Answers.

1. Rebirth.
2. Type.
3. Time, place, action.
4. To show the resolution of conflict.
5. To paint the pictures needed in the minds of the audience; to fill the gaps now filled by technology: props, setting, special effects, etc.
6. To set the scene, give background, extra information, introduce the characters.
7. To break the tension, allow the audience a rest from the drama.
8. A soliloquy is a speech delivered by a central character, purely for the ears of the audience (a kind of thinking aloud).
9. The Porter in *Macbeth*, Falstaff in *Henry V*.
10. Historical sources, Italian and French romantic narratives from the fifteenth century.

THE KEY ELEMENTS OF THE PLAYS

Themes

Structure and plot

Characterisation

Themes

A theme is an overall idea running through a play or novel. It is not the same as a plot or storyline. The theme is the point that is being made by the story; the main idea to take with you when the story is over.

Usually, themes have something to do with a facet of human nature; Shakespeare was particularly interested in exploring human experience. The following themes are recurrent in his plays:

- Love
- Betrayal
- Jealousy
- Partnerships
- Loyalty

The plays are also timeless, which is why people still love Shakespeare today. The themes are still relevant four hundred years after the plays were first performed.

If you are struggling to identify the theme of a play, ask yourself four things:

1   What is this play about?
2   Why has it been written?
3   What was the writer trying to describe/analyse/explore?
4   What is the overall point?

Let us take *Henry V* as an example and apply these four things to the following question.

'*Henry V* is the study of an attempt to identify the human element in the politics of the English monarchy.' Discuss.

Our answers might look something like this:

N O T E S

Structure and plot

Drama is about conflict. Each play follows this pattern:

- an exposition
- some development
- a crisis
- some redevelopment
- a catastrophe
- a denouement

This is a traditional structure which forms the progression of events in a plot, a kind of drama 'formula' which relies on common sense.

The essential conflict in drama can be within an individual – a dilemma faced by a character, a difficult decision to make – or a conflict with others. Clearly the audience has to be made aware that there is a conflict, and have some information about what it concerns.

THINK ABOUT IT

Think about the word 'exposed' when grappling with the idea of exposition. To expose something is to see it clearly so that one can understand it.

- **Exposition** – the revealing of the conflict is called
'Exposition'. Exposition occurs for example in Scene 2 of
The Tempest, when Prospero gives the long narrative
explaining his brother's betrayal, or Scene 1 of *Romeo and
Juliet* with the fight between Capulet and Montague. Often
the Chorus ▶ see p 20 would help with narrative
exposition by giving useful background information, as in
the preliminary to *Romeo and Juliet*:

    Two households, both alike in dignity
    In fair Verona where we lay our scene,
    From ancient grudge break to new mutiny
    Where civil blood makes civil hands unclean

- **Development** – this is usually in Act II, where some plans
will be made by the character or characters to sort out the
conflict. It is too early in the play for any plans to be
conclusive though. Development takes place in *Twelfth
Night*, where Maria and Sir Toby plot to humiliate Malvolio
with the forged letter from Olivia: 'I will drop his way some
obscure epistles of love.'

- **Crisis** – there will be some kind of action as a result of this
planning, usually referred to as the crisis. It normally takes
place in Act III. This is Duncan's murder in *Macbeth*, and
the fight scene in *Romeo and Juliet*.

- **Redevelopment** – following the crisis will be 'redevelopment'.
This is often in Act IV as the new circumstances brought
about by the action of the crisis are dealt with. Act IV of *The
Merchant of Venice* is the court scene, where Antonio is saved
from almost certain death by Portia's skill and judgement.

- **Catastrophe** – we are led through to Act V and the 'catastrophe'
(which originally meant sorting-out, not disaster!). This is the
part where all the events are put into their rightful place and
any misunderstandings are finally ironed out.

- **Denouement** – in which there will be final comment on the catastrophe and what has been learned from the events of the play. Gratiano vows to keep safe 'Nerissa's ring' at the end of *The Merchant of Venice*, showing that he has learned to treasure the one he loves.

HIGHER PERFORMANCE

Any examiner will be seriously impressed with students who refer to dramatic structures in their essays. A good tip would be to use these terms – almost 'drop them in' subtly in your essay on Shakespeare; when you are talking about the murder in *Macbeth*, say something like, 'the plot development moves into crisis as *Macbeth* is drawn deeper into the plot to assassinate Duncan ...'

These dramatic structures were not cast in stone, of course. Although they are most definitely present and a vital part of any dramatic work, they do tend to ebb and flow into one another. The sub-plot denouement may occur in Act IV, giving way for the final main plot denouement in Act V. There may be several crisis moments.

Characterisation

We have seen how Shakespeare worked within certain parameters of expectation in the construction of his plays. He dealt with the creation of character in the same way. Shakespeare used clearly identifiable 'types' of character, which he then manipulated and added a wealth of depth and interest to. His characters are fascinating, complex and lifelike.

Let's look first of all at the stock 'types'; remembering of course that they could often overlap and contain elements of more than one characteristic. The main types are again taken from classical traditional theatre:

- The tragic hero
- The romantic hero
- The villain
- Women
- Comic characters

The tragic hero

The tragic heroes are central male characters in a tragedy.  see p 8. The essential elements are:

– The character needs to hold some kind of elevated status at the outset of the play.

– There needs to be some kind of aberration, or weakness of character (known as the 'fatal flaw').

– This fatal flaw causes the tragic hero to take inevitable steps towards his own downfall from his lofty position, often dragging lots of the other characters along with him.

– At the end of the play, order is restored once the tragic hero is out of the way.

– A sense of fate, or inevitability, or 'Karma' if you like, directs the tragic hero's actions; in other words, you know he will mess up massively, he deserves what is coming, but you still feel a sense of regret that he could be so stupid. You need to get a 'moral' or lesson from the story.

The romantic hero

The romantic hero's role is to be in love – and this is what causes the complication and interest.

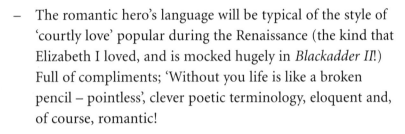

–   He is the male part of the love element in the play; Bassanio, Romeo and Sebastian are all romantic heroes.

–   His function is to love, or be love-lorn. He will tend to be quite serious and not have really witty things to say, or do anything really terrible.

–   The romantic hero's language will be typical of the style of 'courtly love' popular during the Renaissance (the kind that Elizabeth I loved, and is mocked hugely in *Blackadder II*!) Full of compliments; 'Without you life is like a broken pencil – pointless', clever poetic terminology, eloquent and, of course, romantic!

–   The romantic hero doesn't have to die!

There are also the romantic heroines, who form the counterpart to the romantic hero and perform little function other than to be the fuel to his fire, if you like! Miranda and Olivia are good examples from our plays.

The villain

Plays need villains to make life more interesting.

– The villain is the 'baddie'. They wish bad things to happen to the good characters, and they have some measure of success.

– They are always thwarted at the end, to the satisfaction of everyone. They always deserve what they get.

– They are flat, lifeless characters without much substance in the comedies.

– However, they need to have some kind of motivation for their actions otherwise they would just be 'caricatures'.

– Caliban, Tybalt, Shylock, and Malvolio are all examples of villains from our plays.

HIGHER PERFORMANCE

Caliban is a villain of course; he is a savage who attempts to rape the beautiful, innocent Miranda. He repays his master by attempting to overthrow him and regain his island for himself. HOWEVER!!! Isn't it his own island in the first place? And also, he does not understand the enormity of his attempted crime against Miranda as he is an uneducated savage. He is a very good example of a character who is impossible to label simply 'a villain' without careful consideration of his motives and point of view.

Women

Despite the impossibility of Shakespeare using women on stage, it is possible to identify key features:

- Shakespeare had a massive problem when it came to writing female characters. ▶ see p 21

- As female actors were not allowed, it fell to young, pre-pubescent boys to perform the female roles. Thus there are very few strong female leads, and these were almost definitely written with a specific boy actor in mind who would be able to perform them effectively.

- The interesting thing about the female characters in Shakespeare is that in spite of the restrictions he was working under, he always created strong, multi-faceted women. It is the women in the plays who stand out as the really punchy characters.

- Lady Macbeth, Portia, Juliet, Viola – all these are complex, assertive, intelligent women. Shakespeare had a fascination for allowing his female characters to explore the restrictions of their worlds in the same way that he was working under restrictions.

THINK ABOUT IT

Juliet is the strong half of the partnership with Romeo. Her language is powerful, vibrant, eloquent and strong. She initiates the issue of marriage, she takes the lead in sorting out the mess after the deaths of Tybalt and Mercutio, she is the one who takes her own life first. What does Romeo do? Lots of moaning and writhing around and being lovesick and letting everyone else sort out his life for him!

Comic characters

There is always at least one comic character, even in the tragedies. The essential elements are:

– The comic characters say the funny lines.

– They are invariably the butt of the joke.

– They tend to be low-status, such as servants.

– They often have their own subplot which will have some kind of thematic link to the main plot.

– The intentions of the comic characters are always good, if sometimes misguided through ignorance or stupidity.

– One of their functions in the tragedies is partly to comment on the main plot whilst appearing to be totally separate from it.

– Another function is to give the audience a break from the emotionally-charged tension of the main action.

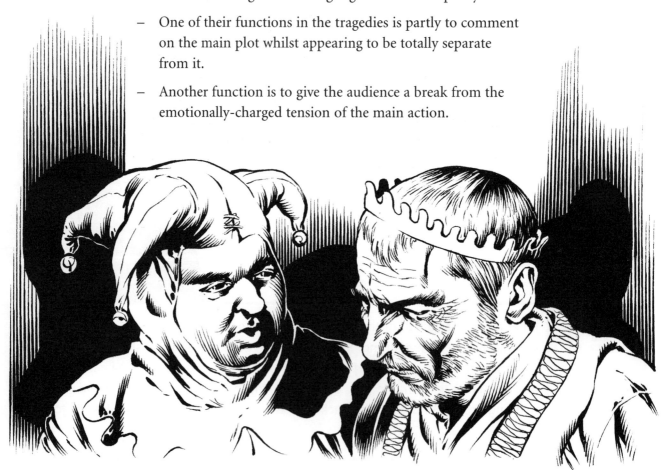

Analysing character

When undertaking any kind of analysis of a character, there are three golden rules to apply.

1. Look at what the character says; their words, use of language ▶ **see pp 40-55**, content, tone. The soliloquies ▶ **see p 23** are vital here because you get everything from the character's heart.

2. Look at what the character does; their actions, how honest they are, what they do compared to what they say, etc.

3. Look at how others react to them and what others say about them. Do honest, trustworthy characters like them? Who are their friends? Who are their enemies?

Personal judgement is involved in any kind of character study. Try to imagine that the character is real. Think about how you would react to that person if you knew them. In the end though, you will hardly ever be required to present a damning indictment or a eulogy for any Shakespearean character. It is, however, very likely that you will be asked to discuss, describe, comment on or consider a character.

HIGHER PERFORMANCE

1 Discuss how a feminist might view the situation of one of the following women;
Portia, Lady Macbeth and Jessica, Shylock's daughter.

2 Who or what is most to blame for the downfall of Macbeth?

3 Why did Shakespeare originally entitle *The Merchant of Venice*, 'Shylock the Jew'?

Quiz

1. Name one essential element of a tragic hero.

2. What is the meaning of the term 'fatal flaw'?

3. Name two romantic heroes from the plays discussed in this book.

4. Who is the villain of *The Merchant of Venice?*

5. Who is the romantic heroine in *The Tempest*?

6. Who in *The Merchant of Venice* dresses as a man in order to enter the world of business and the law?

7. What are the three golden rules of character study?

8. Does a villain ever win at the end of a Shakespearean play?

9. Name the main comic character of *Henry V.*

10. Who is the romantic hero of *The Merchant of Venice?*

THE LANGUAGE OF THE PLAYS

Poetry

Prose

Imagery

OK, so how many people reading this are willing to hold up their hand and admit that they find Shakespeare's language hard to understand?

Would it surprise you if everyone raised their hand to that question, even the teachers, the professors in the universities, the authors of books on Shakespeare? When you think about it, it is not so surprising really. Remember opening your copy of *Romeo and Juliet* at Act I Scene 1:

SAMP: *Gregory, on my word we'll not carry coals.*
GREG: *No, for then we would be colliers.*
SAMP: *I mean, and we be in choler, we'll draw.*
GREG: *Ay, while you live, draw your neck out of collar.*

'What on earth are they talking about?', you think. Your heart sinks, that steel shutter between your ears and your brain comes crashing down, and you're set for a term of your poor teacher bashing as much of the meaning as possible into your skull to get you through your GCSE! Sound familiar?

Then can you explain, perhaps, how it is that the story has stuck? That you know loads about Romeo's character? That you understand why Mercutio dies? That you would be able to write a really good character study of the Nurse? If the language is so difficult, how come we all understand it?

It is more difficult than modern literature because it is old, it is constructed differently, and it uses some unfamiliar words. Shakespeare takes some wading through, and some thinking about. It is some of the most beautiful poetry in the world; worth all the effort, most people who study it think. Books wouldn't be written about Shakespeare's language if it was crystal clear to a modern audience; have you ever seen any books showing you how to understand your local newspaper?

Don't despair. Get through all the hallmarks of Renaissance language (all those thees and thous and hasts and wherefores) and the whole thing becomes much easier. Also, remember that nearly all modern published editions contain some kind of helpful glossary to tell you what the stranger words and phrases mean.

DID YOU KNOW?
The Elizabethans loved playing with words. Courtiers of Elizabeth I and James I actually practised wordplay as a real sport, and it was seen to be a hallmark of genteel breeding.

Poetry

Much of Shakespeare's work is written in poetry.

Each line of his verse has a structure with measurable rhythm and rhyme. He uses imagery such as simile and metaphor and language techniques such as alliteration and enjambement.

Blank verse

Generally, blank verse was used for the important, high status characters, whereas the comic characters, the servants, and the insignificant bits were in prose. It was one way of indicating to the audience the importance of what they were hearing.

Blank verse is a style of poetry. Each line of verse has exactly ten syllables.

Let's look at some examples of famous lines from our chosen plays:

Once more unto the breach, dear friends, once more,
Or close the wall up with our English dead. (Henry V)

If music be the food of love, play on. (Twelfth Night)

All hail, Macbeth! Hail to thee, Thane of Glamis! (Macbeth)

Guess what – these all have ten syllables!

DID YOU KNOW?
The suffix '-ed' was sounded, or pronounced as a separate syllable in the sixteenth century. If Shakespeare didn't want to sound the syllable, he would show it like this:
'Hugg'd and embraced' – there are five syllables here.

The next stage is looking at how the syllables are divided. Generally, we split them up into five that are stressed, or said more powerfully, and five that are unstressed. These stressed and unstressed syllables tend to alternate with each other, and kind of follow the pattern of how the English language is spoken. Here's an example:

> *But soft! What light through yonder window breaks?*
> *It is the east, and Juliet is the sun.*
> *Arise, fair sun, and kill the envious moon,*
> *Who is already sick and pale with grief…*   *(Romeo and Juliet)*

Each pair of syllables, the unstressed followed by the stressed, is called 'an iamb'. There are five 'iambs' in each line of blank verse.

The length of the line of the verse, measured by counting the stresses, is called 'the metre'. 'Metre' originally meant 'a unit of measurement'. When there are five 'units of measurement' or iambs in the line (as there are in the example above), that kind of line is called a 'pentameter', which means five units of measurement.

When the lines of verse do not rhyme all the time, this is called blank verse. Shakespeare constructs his verse into blank verse, using iambic pentameter.

That may have sounded terribly dry, boring and irrelevant, but it is really important.

Having got his basic framework of poetry, Shakespeare played around with it all the time to emphasise meaning and make ideas and language flow. You can spot a bad actor at five paces if they deliver every line of Shakespeare by sticking rigidly to the metre, making it sound clomping and ridiculous.

still awake?

Rhyme

Blank verse is recognisable as poetry because of its structured rhythm and metre. Actual rhyme is more infrequent; the most common rhyme formation consistently employed by Shakespeare was the rhyming couplet, or 'heroic' couplet. Rhyming couplets are often used at the end of a long speech of blank verse, also usually the end of a scene to bring a sense of closure and 'end with a bang'.

Let's look at a couplet to give an illustration of how they work. In *Henry V*, when Henry is attempting to bluff the citizens of Harfleur into surrender by describing all the horrible things his army may do when they eventually take the town, he ends up with a question;

> *What say you? Will you yield, and this avoid?*
> *Or, guilty in defence, be thus destroy'd?*

There is no more striking example of a rhyming couplet used to give closure than the final two lines of *Romeo and Juliet*:

> *For never was a story of more woe*
> *Than this of Juliet, and her Romeo.*

Even the common ordering of the lovers' names is reversed in order that the rhyme can occur here, and charge the ending of the play with the deep emotional impact of the lines.

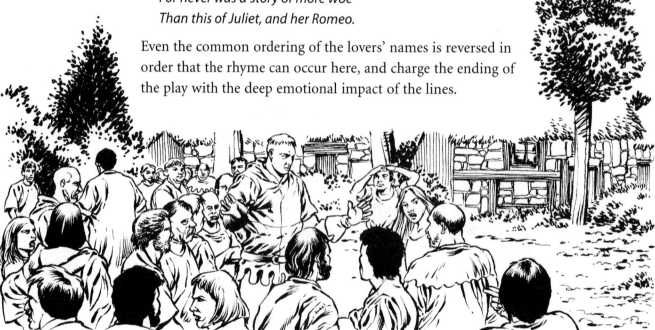

The sonnet

The sonnet form was made popular by a fourteenth century Italian poet named Petrarch who wrote 366 love poems to a woman called Laura (who he never actually spoke to, incidently!). This kind of poem contains conceits which are figurative devices making clever or unlikely comparisons.

A common type of sonnet written in Shakespearean times was a 'blazon' or poem written in praise of a particular woman's beauty by listing particular qualities possessed by said lady. This was not enough for Shakespeare though. When he wrote his sonnets, he included all kinds of complicated and clever ideas around themes like death and nature. Basically, a sonnet is a love poem which is recognisable as a sonnet and not a limerick because:

– it is generally serious in tone
– it is about love
– it has fourteen lines
– the lines are written in iambic pentameter

The rhyme schemes of sonnets vary, but a Shakespearean sonnet can be broken into four pieces. The first three pieces are sections of four lines in length, or quatrains, in which each alternate line rhymes, i.e. abab;

> *Like as the waves make towards the pebbled shore,*
> *So do our minutes hasten to their end;*
> *Each changing place with that which goes before,*
> *In sequent toil all forwards do contend.*

The last two lines consist of heroic couplet as a finisher:

> *And yet to times in hope my verse shalt stand,*
> *Praising thy worth, despite his cruel hand.*

Sonnets in the plays

The most famous example of sonnets used in the plays is the first fourteen-line exchange between Romeo and Juliet in Act I scene 5:

> *If I profane with my unworthiest hand*
> *This holy shrine, the gentle sin is this;*
> *My lips, two blushing pilgrims, ready stand*
> *To smooth that rough touch with a tender kiss.*

This first quatrain opens the dialogue, making a complicated comparison between Juliet and and a holy shrine. What a fancy chat up line!

Juliet's response is ready and quick, showing the equality between them as well as reinforcing the romance by continuing the sonnet form into the second quatrain;

> *Good pilgrim, you do wrong your hand too much*
> *Which mannerly devotion shows in this;*
> *For saints have hands, that pilgrims' hands do touch*
> *And palm to palm, is holy palmer's kiss.*

DID YOU KNOW?

There are three kinds of sonnet: The Petrarchan, or Italian sonnet, which rhymes abba abba cdecde, the Spenserian sonnet, which rhymes abab bcbc cdcd ee; and our Shakespearean sonnet, which rhymes abab cdcd efef gg.

Prose

Prose is much easier to explain and easier to recognise.
Prose is everything that's not poetry. Newsprint, novels
and stories, letters, articles and diaries are written in prose.
We have already mentioned that while blank verse was the
general style, prose was used as the means by which the comic,
lower status characters delivered their lines. This is generally
true, but Shakespeare, who never did anything simply when he
could make it complicated, also used prose as a stylistic
technique.

Prose lacks the formal structure of blank verse, so it was
really useful for showing distress, anxiety, irrational thinking
and lack of control in his high status characters. A really good
example of this is the opening of the fight scene of *Romeo and
Juliet*:

> BEN: I pray thee, good Mercutio, let's retire;
>   The day is hot, the Capels are abroad,
>   And if we meet we shall not 'scape a brawl,
>   For now these hot days is the mad blood stirring.
>
> MER: Thou art like one of those fellows that, when he enters
>   the confines of a tavern, claps me his sword upon the table
>   and says 'God send me no need of thee!' and by the
>   operation of the second cup draws him on the drawer,
>   when indeed there is no need.

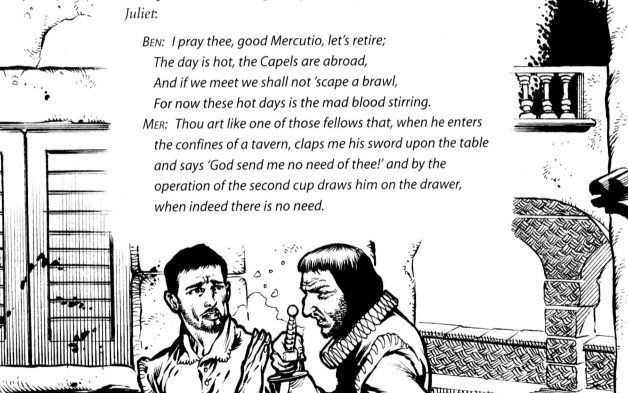

Not only can we physically see the difference between prose and blank verse here but it is also obvious why Shakespeare uses these two styles: Benvolio's measured, calm, rational blank verse is contrasted totally to Mercutio's rambling prose. Instantly, this serves to highlight his agitated state of mind to the audience, and give an indication that he is in a mood for trouble.

Another good example of the metre being used for effect is the scene immediately after Duncan's murder in *Macbeth*; Macbeth and his wife speak in fragmented blank verse to indicate the tension of the situation.

> L. MAC: *I heard the owl scream, and the crickets cry. Did not you speak?*
> MAC: *When?*
> L. MAC: *Now.*
> MAC: *As I descended?*

This highly-charged speech is immediately followed by the Porter, who delivers a whole section of prose:

> *Here's a knocking indeed! If a man were porter of hell-gate,*
> *he should have old turning the key. Knock, knock, knock!*
> *Who's there, i'th'name of Beelzebub?*

DID YOU KNOW?
Dictionaries were not around in the days when Shakespeare was writing. In fact, the first dictionary, written by Samuel Johnson, was not published until the eighteenth century. Therefore there were no standard spellings of words; no common agreement on how any word should be spelt. Imagine how Shakespeare loved that? It was a joy to a poet to have that kind of freedom; sometimes he would spell a word five different ways in one play!

The content and the style break up the fraught tension of the previous scene; there is some bawdy comment about alcohol 'provoking desire and taking away performance' which the audience can laugh at, as well as some ironic comment on the castle gates being a metaphor for the gates of Hell. The function of the Porter, to break the tension and give the audience a bit of a break, is emphasised by his less formal language. ▶ see p 22

KEY CONCEPTS

Blank verse indicates a character's status ✳

Rhyming couplets end scenes ✳

Prose is used by lower-status characters ✳

HIGHER PERFORMANCE

The Captain, who opens *Macbeth* with all the information the audience needs about this brave and fierce warrior, delivers his lines in beautiful blank verse, full of poetic imagery; loads of similes and metaphors and generally 'high' style language. As a character he is merely an information-giver, never seen again. He delivers his one speech in a form unsuited to his character status because of the importance of the information, and where it comes in the play. It is the content of the words that deserve the blank verse, not the status of the character delivering them. There are lots of other examples of this technique in the plays.

Imagery

An image is a picture. Pictorial images, photographic images, physical images; they are all things we can see. When a poet writes, he or she is using language to work on your senses, not just your cognitive understanding. A poet wants you to feel the emotion, sense the feeling, and see the picture they are trying to create in their work. Imagery is the technique used in order to do this; it adds another dimension of meaning to the surface, literal meaning. Poets use similes and metaphors to create an image.

Simile

A simile is a poetic or linguistic device. It works by comparing something to something else, and usually is flagged by the words 'as' or 'like'. Similes have become so common that many have become clichés in our language;

Metaphor

A metaphor works in exactly the same way as a simile, but is sometimes harder to spot because it eliminates the explicit comparison and claims that something is something else:

Shakespeare used imagery all the time. The images were often linked to the story and especially the theme; in other words, there would be a distinct set of images running through a particular play to emphasise the mood he was trying to create. For example, images of money and finance, chance and hazard occur frequently in *The Merchant of Venice* to support the theme of love being a commodity or business deal:

In Belmont is a lady richly left

Look on beauty,
And you shall see 'tis purchased by the weight

Another example is *Macbeth*, which is littered with references to blood, sleeplessness, nocturnal animals, storms and the supernatural; clearly reinforcing the theme of nature being turned upside down by Macbeth's murder of the king:

> *The night has been unruly: where we lay,*
> *Our chimneys were blown down, and, as they say,*
> *Lamentings heard i'th'air, strange screams of death,*
> *And prophesying with accents terrible*
> *Of dire combustion and confused events*
> *New hatched to th' woeful time. The obscure bird*
> *Clamoured the livelong night: some say, the earth*
> *Was feverous and did shake*

Sometimes the imagery is created by simple repetition of an idea, such as continual references to sea storms and shipwrecks in *The Tempest*, or the contrast of opposites in *Romeo and Juliet*.

The other technique is to use simile and metaphor, i.e. creating an image by comparison to reinforce meaning.

> *My mind is tossing on the ocean* (Antonio, *The Merchant of Venice*)

> *When we have match'd our rackets to these balls,*
> *We will in France, by God's grace, play a set*
> *Shall strike his father's crown into the hazard.* (Henry, *Henry V*)

> *Look like the innocent flower,*
> *But be the serpent under't.* (Lady Macbeth, *Macbeth*)

Much of the language of the plays was confined by poetic conventions of imagery, rhythm and metre such as we have seen above. Still, the characters sound realistic; go to see any production of a Shakespeare play and you will believe in the language; it won't sound like poetry being delivered. This is because Shakespeare mirrored the language of life in his work;

the pace, rhythm and metre of the iambic pentameter is the closest approximation to spoken English there is. Also, everyone uses similes and metaphors all the time, which is why so many have become clichéd in our language. Shakespeare can in the truest sense be known as 'a poet of the people' who wrote in a language everyone can relate to.

HIGHER PERFORMANCE

A really good technique for getting to grips with a text is to go through and find all the images on a particular theme. The idea of contrasts and conflict of opposites in *Romeo and Juliet* is an excellent one to start with. There is actually a literary term for this kind of imagery, known as 'a conceit'. Conceit means an elaborate image or far-fetched comparison, and was really popular amongst Shakespeare and his contemporaries. Here are a few from *Romeo and Juliet* to start you off:

What, drawn, and talk of peace?   (Tybalt)

Why then, O brawling love, O loving hate, …
O heavy lightness, serious vanity …
Feather of lead, bright smoke, cold fire, sick health,
Still-waking sleep that is not what it is!   (Romeo)

I will withdraw; but this intrusion shall
Now seeming sweet, convert to bitt'rest gall.   (Tybalt)

HIGHER PERFORMANCE

Now you know all about poetic language and structures, let's go back to the first play you ever studied; our guess is it's probably *Romeo and Juliet*!

Taking each of the following examples from *Romeo and Juliet* in turn, describe the effect of it and the reasons Shakespeare has chosen to use it.

1

> *Eyes, look your last.*
> *Arms, take your last embrace! And lips, O you*
> *The doors of breath, seal with a righteous kiss*
> *A dateless bargain to engrossing Death.*
> *Come, bitter conduct, come unsavoury guide,*
> *Thou desperate pilot now at one run on*
> *The dashing rocks thy seasick weary bark.*
> *Here's to my love! [He drinks.] O true apothecary,*
> *Thy drugs are quick. Thus with a kiss I die.*

2

> *Madam, the guests are come, supper served up, you called,*
> *my young lady asked for, the Nurse cursed in the pantry, and*
> *everything in extremity. I must hence to wait, I beseech you*
> *follow straight.*

3

> *If I profane, with my unworthiest hand*
> *This holy shrine, the gentle sin is this:*
> *My lips, two blushing pilgrims, ready stand*
> *To smooth that rough touch with a tender kiss.*

4

> *Good pilgrim, you do wrong your hand too much,*
> *Which mannerly devotion shows in this;*
> *For saints have hands that pilgrims' hands do touch,*
> *And palm to palm is holy palmers' kiss.*

Quiz

1. What kind of writer was Shakespeare primarily?

2. Name the type of poems he wrote.

3. Which kind of character normally speaks in blank verse?

4. Which kind of character normally used prose?

5. Think of some examples of modern day prose in use.

6. How many syllables are there in a line of iambic pentameter?

7. What does 'metre' mean?

8. What comparative conjunctions normally are used in a simile?

9. Does blank verse rhyme always/sometimes/never?

10. Did Shakespeare stick to rigid blank verse in the plays?

Answers

1. Poet.
2. Sonnets.
3. High-status character/important to the plot.
4. Low status character/minor.
5. Novels, newspapers, advertisements, magazines, instruction books...
6. Ten.
7. Unit of measurement.
8. Like/as.
9. Sometimes.
10. Hardly ever.

First recorded date 1595

Classed as a tragedy originally, now known as a 'tragicomedy' or 'dark' comedy

Romeo and Juliet are the children of families with a long history of enmity who meet and fall in love. Their short-lived romance is conducted in secret and is ended with the eventual death of both due to a series of tragic misunderstandings. Their death unites their respective families into sworn peace.

Plot

The 'Chorus' see p 20 which introduces this play gives the audience a brief outline of the story they are about to see. The actor playing the Chorus is given some strong opening lines with which to engage interest straight away:

> *Two households, both alike in dignity*
> *In fair Verona, where we lay our scene*
> *From ancient grudge break to new mutiny*

The two households are the Capulets and the Montagues, both wealthy and powerful families occupying equal status in fifteenth-century Verona. For some unknown reason, they have been rivals for many years with periodic outbursts of violence.

Juliet is the fourteen-year-old daughter of Lord and Lady Capulet, and Romeo is the only child of the Montagues. They meet and fall in love, and are dismayed when they discover that their families are enemies. In spite of these difficult circumstances they are determined to marry.

Romeo becomes involved in a fight between his best friend Mercutio and Juliet's fiery cousin Tybalt. Tybalt kills Mercutio by accident and Romeo, beside himself with rage, seeks out Tybalt and kills him. He is banished from Verona as a punishment. At the same time, the Capulets arrange for Juliet to be married to a young nobleman. In desperation she seeks help from Friar Lawrence. He gives her a potion which will make her appear dead, buying enough time for Romeo to sneak her away. Unfortunately, the message sent to Romeo with this plan never arrives and he hears only that his wife is dead. He poisons himself just before Juliet wakes from her sleep and she then stabs herself with Romeo's dagger. The Capulets and Montagues realise that their fighting is to blame for this tragedy and are reconciled at last.

DID YOU KNOW?

The recent film with Claire Danes and Leonardo DiCaprio is not the only famous version of *Romeo and Juliet*; back in the 1960s, *West Side Story* was a hugely successful musical film version of the play set in New York.

Main Themes

The generation gap

This theme is clearly central to the plot – Romeo and Juliet try to overcome the differences between their parents; they have a different notion of marriage; they are at odds with the older generation; age is a constant allusion throughout the play.

The older and younger generation form two distinct groups in this play. However, older in this sense definitely does not appear to mean 'wiser'; Lord and Lady Capulet, Friar Lawrence and the Nurse all make dreadful mistakes and contribute greatly to the tragedy by their behaviour. By the end of the play there is a sense that the younger generation has been sacrificed to the stupidity of their elders.

The nature of opposites

The whole play is about fighting between opposite forces; Montague against Capulet, youth against age, romance against cynicism, pragmatism against hedonism. There are constant references to opposites in the language, particularly as spoken by Romeo.

Love

Romantic love is the central idea, but other kinds of love are a constant factor; idealised, courtly love such as that Romeo holds for Rosaline; a parent's love for their child; a child's sense of love and duty towards their parents; love between friends; love for honour and your family.

Youth and maturity

Romeo and Juliet are both constantly referred to as children by those around them, and both do a great deal of growing up during the course of the play. Maturity involves making independent decisions, being strong and brave, recognising obstacles, and doing right by those around you.

Youth and maturity is a strong theme. Juliet's age is highlighted from the outset; she is old enough to be a marriage bargain for her father, and yet is treated as a child. Her maturity comes across very clearly in her directness with Romeo. It is she who brings up the subject of marriage to Romeo, remember!

She sends the Nurse to Romeo, she goes to Friar Lawrence and demands his help, and she stabs herself rather than remain alive. These are not the actions of a child, in spite of being 'yet a stranger to this world'.

Romeo, however, is marked out as youthful from the beginning. His infatuation over Rosaline is immature affection. His selfish behaviour causes concern to his parents and his friends. He is like a sulky teenager at the start of the play!

Only when he hears of Juliet's death does his behaviour change. He transforms into a determined, forceful man. Buying the poison from the apothecary and killing Paris rather than letting him bar the way to Juliet's tomb mark out his transformation. He even refers to this himself – 'tempt not a desperate man'.

Structure

Exposition

The Chorus gives the background, speedily followed by the fight which illustrates the enmity between Capulet and Montague. Romeo being besotted with Rosaline places him as a young, silly boy with little to think of other than himself. Juliet's passive acquiescence to her parents shows her to be meek, pliable and dominated by others older than herself.

Development

Romeo and Juliet meet and exchange vows. Tybalt promises to avenge Romeo for his apparent slight of the Capulet honour.

Crisis

Romeo and Juliet marry in secret. Tybalt kills Mercutio, Romeo kills Tybalt and flees Verona. Juliet is betrothed to Paris.

Redevelopment

Friar Lawrence hatches the plan with Juliet to fake her death. Romeo gets the wrong message from Balthazar and ends his own life; Juliet wakes from her drugged sleep and kills herself.

Catastrophe

Friar Lawrence explains all to the Prince and the grieving families.

Denouement

The Prince points to the shared guilt of Capulet and Montague in perpetrating this joint tragedy. The families are finally reconciled.

One of the most remarkable facets of this play is the timespan.
Look at the diary below. Time is a major factor in the play, and a sense of
pace and urgency dominates throughout.

Sunday

9.a.m. Rosaline turns Romeo down.
9.p.m. With Mercutio, Romeo and Benvolio gatecrash the
Capulet's masked ball. Romeo and Juliet meet and instantly
fall for each other, then realise that their families are sworn
enemies.
12.00 a.m. Romeo woos Juliet under her balcony.

Monday

6.00 a.m. Romeo asks Friar Lawrence to marry them.
12.00 p.m. Romeo and Juliet meet at Friar Lawrence's and
are married secretly.
3.00 p.m. Tybalt kills Mercutio, Romeo kills Tybalt. Romeo
is banished from Verona.
6.00 p.m. Juliet discovers that Tybalt is dead and Romeo
banished. She sends the Nurse to find Romeo.
7.00 p.m. Capulet offers Juliet's hand in marriage to Paris.
10.00p.m. The Nurse stops Romeo from killing himself.
Friar Lawrence urges Romeo to spend the night with Juliet
before his exile to Mantua.

Tuesday

5.00 a.m. Romeo leaves Juliet for his exile in Mantua
11.00 a.m Juliet refuses to marry Paris, but the wedding is
arranged anyway. Friar Lawrence gives her a drug that will
fake her death for 42 hours to avoid the marriage. They
plan her escape to Mantua.
6.00 p.m. Juliet's marriage to Paris is brought forward to
Wednesday.
11.00 p.m. Juliet takes the drug.

Wednesday

8.00 a.m. Nurse finds Juliet for dead. Friar Lawrence
organises the funeral with the Capulets.
11.00 a.m. Balthasar arrives in Mantua to tell Romeo that
Juliet is dead. Romeo leaves for Verona.
9.00 p.m. Romeo kills Paris. Romeo goes into Juliet's tomb,
kisses her one last time and poisons himself. Juliet comes
round, finds Romeo dead and stabs herself to death in
despair.

Thursday

8.00 a.m. The Capulets and Montagues realise that the
tragedy has been as a result of their feuding and reach a
reconciliation.

Closing Thoughts

The Prince is the dominant figure at the beginning and end of the play. He directs the action by threatening severe punishments to both families if the feud between them does not end. He presides over the tragic ending, commenting on the judgement that fate has visited all by the deaths of Romeo, Juliet, Mercutio and Tybalt.

The fight at the beginning of the play sets the tone of violence and highlights the bitter and futile nature of the feud between the families. It is 'bred of an airy word', started by servants who show themselves to be frivolous and petty characters and is quickly fuelled into outright battle by the 'fiery' Tybalt's hatred of peace: 'I hate the word, as I hate Hell, all Montagues and thee'.

Romeo and Juliet are the central characters and the play is their love story. However, they are seen together only four times: at the masque, the love scene on Juliet's balcony, their marriage and the morning that Romeo flees Verona. These moments are captivating because of the beautiful, lyrical nature of the language they use. The scenes stand out as brief but powerful in contrast to the disarray and hatred around them. Also, there is no subplot to this play, meaning that the love story has sole and dominant focus throughout.

The central scene of the play is the fighting of Act III Scene 1. This scene changes the course of the play from a gentle romantic comedy into a tragedy. This scene also marks the exit of two dominant characters, Tybalt and Mercutio. When Mercutio announces his refusal to stomach Romeo's apparent cowardice; 'Oh calm, dishonourable, vile submission!' the action takes an abrupt spiral into tragedy. It is from here that time takes on a desperate sense of urgency; Juliet is sped towards a second marriage, the message to Romeo is delayed, Romeo takes the poison just one moment too soon.

Written 1599

The young King of England is anxious to prove his suitability for Kingship. He declares war with France to win back land taken in a previous battle. He shows himself to be a brave and honourable King, and successfully wins the war; sealing further the alliance with France by marrying the French King's daughter Katherine.

Plot

This play forms part of the 'history cycle' of plays; one of ten that Shakespeare wrote in which he chronicled the period of English history from the fourteenth to the sixteenth century. The story of *Henry V* is central to this cycle both chronologically and in its content. The plays surrounding it tell of the upheaval and political unrest in England in that time, highlighting the strength and order of Henry's rule.

From previous plays in the cycle we are aware that Henry has led a wild and reckless youth. He is well known for his 'playboy' lifestyle and many worry about his ability to be a strong ruler. In *Henry IV Part 1*, this Henry is always in the company of the lecherous, drunken gambler Falstaff.

However, fears are allayed by the reformed character he presents as king. He is a thoughtful young man who takes his

position as ruler of England very seriously. He feels strongly
that he is rightful ruler of France, and after taking advice from
associates, decides to invade France and demand the crown.
When French ambassadors arrive with an insulting message
which refer to his previous boyish behaviour, he becomes
enraged and determines to mount an attack on France and win
the crown.

In spite of overwhelming difficulties, he succeeds in his
mission. Although the French army number five-to-one against
the English, Henry's eloquent rallying speech to his men and
fearsome behaviour in battle prove to be the deciding factors in
winning the war against France. The French king agrees to a
treaty whereby Henry will marry his daughter Katherine and
thus ensure heirdom to the throne of France.

THINK ABOUT IT

Katherine and Henry have never appeared together before the proposal scene
and she is very quiet throughout Henry's proposal. Does she want to marry him
or is she aware that she must do what her father wishes? Is she a willing fiancée
or a pawn in a political alliance?

Main Themes

Patriotism

This theme is one which was not lost on the British government when they commissioned a production of *Henry V* during the Second World War to stir up nationalistic fervour. There are many references to the bravery of the British people; especially in the famous speeches Henry makes to his men at Harfleur and Agincourt. He rallies them by reminding them from what brave and noble stock they come.

The inclusion of the four captains – English, Scots, Welsh and Irish – is an indication of the idea of British patriotism rather than English. Coming from a turbulent history of arguments over power and status between England and all three Celtic neighbours, it is interesting to note how Shakespeare joined all four forces in a statement of unity.

The nature of kingship

Henry is determined to be a good and just ruler and we see this right from the beginning to the end of the play. He makes sure that he can claim right on his side when he begins the war, shows mercy to the French people he vanquishes and ensures an honourable and just peace. To him, being a good king means that he has to put the wellbeing of his people before his own comfort and safety. He has to be the opposite of the fast living young man he was in *Henry IV Part 1*. We see the night before Agincourt that he is a person too. He goes out in disguise to find out what the common soldiers think of him. He also bemoans his lot as king since it brings him no rest or comfort.

The history plays deal with the idea of figure of state, or divine ruler; Richard II thought of himself as more divine in his office than human. Henry is more earthy; he embodies the conflict of man and ruler. A striking lesson for him is when his three erstwhile friends, Cambridge, Scroop and Grey are brought before him for treason. The man Henry is devastated

by this treachery but the king Henry has to act for his country. His tirade against Scroop is about his personal feeling of betrayal by a friend.

War

The horror and injustice of war is concentrated on at various points in the play, for example during the battle of Agincourt the French raid the baggage train and kill the young boys who are attending it. This, as Fluellen points out, is against the rules of moral warfare. Also, in his attempt to win Harfleur when his force are unable to break through the walls, Henry paints a grisly and bloodthirsty picture of the horrible acts that men will commit in a war. We also see that for some people, war can be seen as a money spinner. At the beginning of the play the Archbishops of Canterbury and Ely encourage Henry to declare war on France in order to ensure that the church will not lose money. The characters of Nimm, Bardolph and Pistol all join the army in order to loot France of its riches for their own personal gain. These characters are shown as cowards, cheats and villains.

DID YOU KNOW?
Our modern 'two-fingered gesture' dates back to the battle of Agincourt. English bowmen needed the two fingers on their right hand to pull back their bowstrings, and if the French captured them, they would cut off these two fingers so that they would never fire an arrow again. By waving two fingers at the French, the English were taunting them with their firepower and the gesture has survived to the present day.

Structure

Exposition

This happens during Act I which establishes Henry's concern with winning the throne of France, and gaining justification for doing so. The French Dauphin's insult reminds everyone what Henry was like in the earlier plays, and gives him a challenge to meet. He has to prove himself worthy to be a king.

Development

This happens during Act II with the introduction of the comic characters, Henry's old drinking companions from his days as Prince. Scene 2 introduces the traitors. Henry's response to them shows that integrity and loyalty have now become paramount to him. His actions prove him to be the strong king.

Crisis

Act III shows the takeover of Harfleur, Henry's first victory in France. The rest of this Act is concerned with his soldiers.

Redevelopment

The battle of Agincourt shows Henry brilliantly rallying his troops with his powerful speech to them. It gives further confirmation of his suitability for kingship.

Catastrophe

Act V is another very short Act, in which the title to France is ensured, and Henry woos the king's daughter.

Denouement

There is no real denouement in this play; the events take precedence over spoken musings.

**Closing
Thoughts**

The story of *Henry V* is a reasonably accurate historical account. It is markedly different from the other history plays, and from many of the plays discussed here, because it is about action, not character.

The storyline and the sequence of events are the predominant focus. Henry is the central character obviously; his character is simple and straightforward, easy to work out. The other characters are merely 'sketched'; there is no other detailed depiction of character. This is extremely unusual for Shakespeare.

The plot concerns the decision and action of Henry in challenging his right to be king of France. It deals with the decision-making process, the fall of some traitors, the battles in France, the victory and the wooing of Katherine. We can see from the fact that the first and last Acts are so brief, that Shakespeare intended this play to be about actions, not long discussions. Maybe one reason why the Chorus has such a dominant role in this play is to do with the fact that battle scenes take centre-stage and Shakespeare had to apologise for not being able to make them as realistic as he would have liked!

N
O
T
E
S

Henry is certainly the main character in this play. We see him graduate from being a playboy figure as he was in *Henry IV Part 1* to being an inspiring, just and generous monarch. He has to put aside many of the comforts of the common man which he enjoyed in his youth, for the greater good of his country. Henry is shown to be brave, honest and noble, not afraid to make tough personal decisions and lead his men from the front. Within the play he has to turn his back on his old friends in order to prove himself a credible king.

We also see both sides of the war. We see much bravery and heroism and the bond between soldiers. We also see the cruelty and selfishness that war can bring about in men.

The play is not without comedy, principally provided through the remarkable character of Captain Fluellen. His constant references to his learning and the advice he gives to others regarding the conduct of war are often amusing. For example, he treats Gower to a long, loud lecture as to the value of silence in a military camp!

Above all, *Henry V* is the study of a man's attempt to become an ideal Christian king.

Written 1599

Duke Orsino is in love with Olivia. Viola, disguised as a boy, is employed as messenger for them but falls in love with Orsino herself. Olivia falls in love with Viola's brother Sebastian. Despite the ensuing confusion, the couples are eventually paired off, to the satisfaction of the audience.

Plot

All the conventions of Elizabethan comedy are strictly adhered to in this elaborate comedy of mistaken identity.

Duke Orsino is in love with the Countess Olivia. She refuses to marry because she has vowed to mourn her dead brother for seven years. However, Orsino is not put off by this and continues to try his best with her.

Meanwhile, the twins Viola and Sebastian have been separated by a shipwreck. Both believe the other to be dead. Viola disguises herself as a boy (called 'Cesario') and goes to work for Orsino; he puts her to work as ambassador for him with Olivia. However, Olivia gets very attracted to 'Cesario' and sends her bad-tempered and miserable servant Malvolio with a message for 'him'.

When she receives this message, Viola realises what is

happening. In the meantime though, she has become attracted to Orsino though he does not know this – he thinks she is a boy – 'Cesario'.

Viola also has trouble to face from Sir Andrew Aguecheek, a stupid man who is living in Olivia's court, spending all his money on entertaining Sir Toby Belch who tells him that Olivia loves him and soon will agree to marry him. When he finds out that Olivia is attracted to 'Cesario' a fight is arranged between Sir Andrew and 'Cesario' by Sir Toby.

Viola's brother Sebastian arrives with his rescuer Antonio, deadly enemy of Orsino. When Olivia sees him she thinks he is 'Cesario' and marries him, which he agrees to because he thinks she is very beautiful. He is seen by Sir Andrew and Sir Toby who attack him, also thinking he is 'Cesario'.

Eventually all the confusion is sorted out. Brother and sister are reunited, Orsino realises that he is in love with Viola, Sir Toby marries the servant Maria, and Malvolio is released from the 'dark room' he had been locked in as a punishment for his unreasonable behaviour.

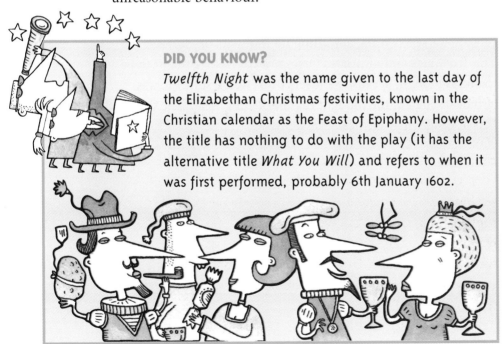

DID YOU KNOW?
Twelfth Night was the name given to the last day of the Elizabethan Christmas festivities, known in the Christian calendar as the Feast of Epiphany. However, the title has nothing to do with the play (it has the alternative title *What You Will*) and refers to when it was first performed, probably 6th January 1602.

Main Themes

Love

Orsino loves Olivia in the kind of idealised, courtly passionate way already remarked upon and mocked in *Romeo and Juliet*. The romance is doomed to failure from the start because Orsino appears to care far more about himself in the partnership than he does about the supposed object of his affections.

Viola loves Orsino in a removed, distant kind of way; she has to, considering that she spends the majority of the play in disguise! Her love is grounded in the real man; she has the chance to get to know him by observation, as he gets fond of her before the romantic attachment can be revealed. She is patient and long-suffering, enduring her situation because she loves this man who doesn't know she exists. The suggestion is that this is the kind of love which warrants rewarding.

Olivia loves 'Cesario' and then Sebastian in a gutsy, passionate, love-at-first-sight kind of way; she gets to marry Sebastian almost before he has time to draw breath!

Both Olivia and Viola love their brothers deeply. Olivia is so distraught at the death of her brother that she vows to remain celibate for seven years, admitting no thoughts of marriage. This frustrates and infuriates Orsino of course! He ought to be thankful though, because he meets Viola as a result! Viola is also devastated at the thought that her twin is dead. She wishes herself dead when she hears the news.

Festivity

If the title of the play is a reference to the date of the first performance, the link to Yuletide festivities and the pursuit of immediate pleasure is clear. Ideas about enjoying life while you can, eating, drinking, dancing and generally 'making hay while the sun shines' are recurrent and abiding.

Sir Toby Belch is the embodiment of this 'live for the moment' attitude towards life; an interesting contrast to his niece at the start, although she betrays some rather impulsive qualities of her own later on! He lives for the ale, his flirtation with Maria and his plot to marry Olivia to his friend Sir Andrew Aguecheek. In recommending this gentleman, Sir Toby judges him as a prize catch because he is tall and a good dancer. Evidently aesthetics and partying are his principal concerns!

The creation of Malvolio is a huge stab at the Puritans, extreme Protestants who wanted the theatres closed because they were 'ungodly'. Clearly Shakespeare would have loved them! Incidentally they were also against public houses, so most of the population were against them! Malvolio is a foil to Sir Toby's drinking and partying until the early hours and so has to be brought low to be punished for his miserable attitude to life.

Structure

This is such a complicated play that to go through it chronologically in order to make some sense of the structure will only confuse even more! We are far better off considering each section/plot and then looking at how they link together:

The opening storyline concerns the Duke Orsino and Countess Olivia. They are the nobility, the aristocracy of the play. They each have a court, which gives two bases for the action to move between. They also have groups of attendants who provide the subplot and the comedy: Sir Toby Belch, Sir Andrew Aguecheek, Maria, Fabian and Feste, and Malvolio.

At the same time, the shipwreck of Sebastian and Viola provides the central plot. Viola's entrance at Orsino's court gives the connection there, more so when she falls in love with him. Her role is central to the structure, as she is employed as go-between for Orsino with Olivia. Olivia needs to meet Viola so that she can fall in love with 'Cesario'.

This is pure comedy of confusion and mistaken identity – within strict boundaries, of course. The audience is never led to feel that the action is out of control, and there is always a sense that discovery and return to order is just around the corner.

Exposition

Concerns Orsino declaring love for Olivia and her refusal to commit romantically. The shipwreck separates Sebastian and Viola.

Development

Viola disguises herself as a boy and takes employment with Orsino. She discovers that she is beginning to have feelings for him. Sir Toby Belch is infuriated with Olivia's decision to be in mourning.

Crisis

Olivia declares her love for Viola ('Cesario'). Sir Andrew Aguecheek challenges Cesario to a duel. Sebastian enters and is attacked by Sir Andrew.

Redevelopment

Olivia mistakes Sebastian for 'Cesario' and the two are married. Malvolio is imprisoned for his strange behaviour.

Catastrophe

The truth of Sebastian and Viola's identity is finally discovered and the two are reunited. Malvolio is released.

Denouement

Three couples are finally correctly paired off.

Closing Thoughts

When we look at *Twelfth Night* in more detail, it is a revealing play that really gives us an insight into what was going on in the Elizabethan era. The play itself conforms to the conventions of Elizabethan romantic comedy, with the typical stock comic characters, the killjoy, the lovers, the twins, the disguise and the confusion. Shakespeare's audience were well aware of these elements and knew exactly what to expect when they came to see the play. However, Shakespeare showed himself to be something of a satirist, taking the mickey out of the Puritans, and making references to topical happenings, such as the tremendous seafaring and voyages of exploration that England and her European neighbours were undertaking.

DID YOU KNOW?
When Fabian says that Sir Andrew has 'sailed into the north of my lady's opinion, where you will hang like an icicle on a Dutchman's beard' he is referring to the Dutch navigator William Barents (d.1597). Barents piloted three Dutch expeditions between 1594-6 to the Arctic in search of the Northeast Passage, a shipping route connecting the Atlantic and Pacific oceans, and very important as a trade route.

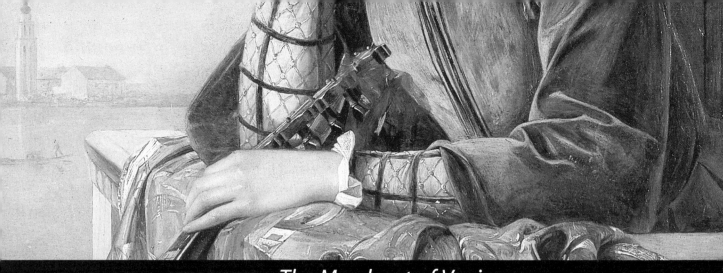

Written around 1600

Shylock the moneylender agrees to lend money to his arch enemy Antonio in return for a pound of flesh if Antonio is unable to pay by the agreed date. Although a joke bargain originally, Shylock decides to pursue his legal right after suffering abuse at the hands of Antonio's friends. He is eventually defeated in court due to a legal technicality and retreats, totally broken, at the end of the play.

Plot

Antonio is a rich Venetian merchant. His closest friend Bassanio asks him for a large loan to give him money to woo a beautiful heiress, Portia. In order to get this money in cash, Antonio has to get a loan from a Jewish moneylender. In Venice at that time, this was the only way of getting loans; the Jewish population of Venice were allowed only a few trades and this was one of them. Christians were not allowed to lend money for financial gain. Jews were despised by Christian Venetian society and had to live in a separate quarter of the town, shut away from the rest of the residents.

Antonio has clearly made his disapproval of Shylock the moneylender very obvious in the past, as Shylock remembers it in detail. However, he agrees to lend Antonio the money free of interest, but in return for a pound of Antonio's flesh if the money is not returned when it is due. Antonio leaps on this 'joke' bargain; he is sure that some merchant ships he owns will soon return and give him plenty of money to repay the debt.

In the meantime, Bassanio goes to Belmont and secures the marriage with Portia. When they hear news that Antonio's ships have not come in and that Shylock is demanding his bond, they return to Venice to help; Portia does this secretly by disguising herself as a young lawyer. The Venetian court can do nothing to help Antonio, and Shylock is determined to have his pound of flesh. One of Antonio's friends has just run away with Shylock's daughter and a large sum of money, so he feels very bitterly towards Antonio and all Christians. He wants revenge. It is Portia who saves the day. She tells Shylock that he can have his bond, but that he must cut off only one pound of flesh exactly, neither more nor less; and that if he fails, his life and all his goods will be 'confiscate'. This is clearly impossible, and Shylock is beaten. The play ends happily for everyone except the Jew, who loses everything.

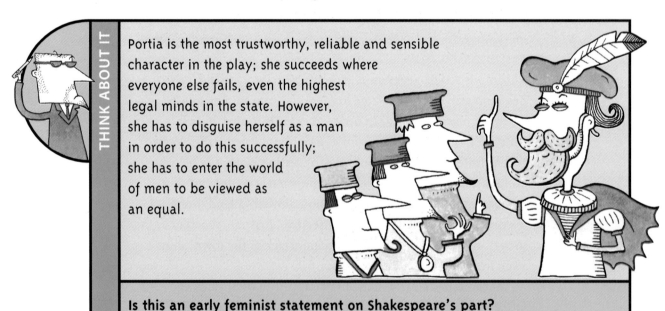

THINK ABOUT IT

Portia is the most trustworthy, reliable and sensible character in the play; she succeeds where everyone else fails, even the highest legal minds in the state. However, she has to disguise herself as a man in order to do this successfully; she has to enter the world of men to be viewed as an equal.

Is this an early feminist statement on Shakespeare's part?

N
O
T
E
S

Main Themes

Revenge and betrayal

Shylock betrays Antonio by turning the apparent 'joke' bond into something far more sinister. Antonio has treated Shylock abominably in the past, so Shylock's act is one of revenge for past insults. However he also claims that he is wreaking revenge upon Antonio for all acts committed by Christians, especially Lorenzo's elopement with his daughter, Jessica. Jessica betrays her father and her religion in her elopement with a Christian.

In return, Antonio's revenge upon Shylock is equally vicious. Once he has regained power, he demands that Shylock renounce his religion; a startlingly cruel act.

Portia and Nerissa have some fun with revenge when they set up their respective partners with the ring plot of Act V. Bassanio and Gratiano betray them by 'giving away' the rings. The women set up the scheme in order to test out their men's fidelity and loyalty and also to teach them a valuable lesson.

Money

The theme of finance is dominant in the action and the language. The main plot is initiated around the idea of money; Bassanio needing a loan, Antonio backing by borrowing himself. Bassanio also thinks that money equals happiness; he wants the 'richly left' Portia predominantly because she is well off. Antonio proves at the beginning and the end of the play that money is not the route to happiness; he is a rich merchant with a miserable life.

Legality and natural law

Shylock uses the letter of the law in order to follow his act of revenge as far as he does. Of course the Venetian legal system appears ludicrous to a modern Western audience, but there is a sense of balance in the fact that this bond has been agreed to and signed by both parties. What is being broken is the idea of 'natural law'.

N
O
T
E
S

Natural law is that sense of humanity, of essential rightness and fair play which tells us morally what is right and what is wrong. In seeking to take the life of another human being, Shylock is breaking moral, natural law even though the official legal system is supporting his claim.

Portia is another victim of this official law. Her father, for all the right reasons, has decreed that his casket game will be the instrument by which her husband is selected. This takes no account of her own feelings, her own choice, her own ability to decide for herself; and she is powerless to do anything about it. She is a lucky girl in that she happens to be attracted to the man who chooses the correct casket!

Different kinds of bond, agreement or promise

The bond between Antonio and Shylock is the major plot device. There are several other bonds or ideas of bonds in the play: the bond and ties of marriage, the bond of friendship, the bond between parent and child. These relationship bonds are concerned with duty, moral responsibility, fairness and what is right and wrong within that relationship. Does Bassanio abuse the bond of friendship between him and Antonio? Does Jessica betray the duties of the daughter in her actions against Shylock, or does he deserve it for his tyrannous behaviour?

Structure

Exposition

Antonio's restlessness is discussed with his concerned friends. Bassanio entreats Antonio for financial help to win the hand of the heiress Portia and Antonio enters the 'bond' with Shylock.

Development

Bassanio wins Portia in the casket challenge. Jessica and Lorenzo plot their elopement and theft of Shylock's money.

Crisis

Shylock discovers his daughter has eloped with a Christian. Antonio learns of the failure of his financial gamble and the embittered Shylock demands that Antonio forfeit his pound of flesh.

Redevelopment

Portia disguises herself as a lawyer and follows Bassanio back to Venice, where she saves Antonio from Shylock's mercilessness. Shylock leaves the scene a broken man; penniless and under oath to convert to Christianity.

Catastrophe

Portia and Nerissa test the fidelity of their lovers with the ring plot. Antonio learns that his venture has succeeded, and is once again a wealthy man.

Denouement

All reflect on the lessons they have learned. Antonio is as silent and isolated at the end of the play as he was at the start.

Closing Thoughts

There are several plots running through this play; some are more subordinate than others, but all are closely linked by the idea of revenge. The plots are:

- Shylock and Antonio and their bond, which forms the central plot of dramatic action

- Portia, Bassanio and the caskets gives us the love story

- Lorenzo, Jessica and the elopement brings in the idea of betrayal

- The test of the rings between Portia and Bassanio and Nerissa and Gratiano echoes ideas of testing love, measuring its worth in monetary value, and betrayal

This play is a romantic comedy; however, it narrowly escapes being described as a tragedy. Since the atrocities of Hitler and the Nazis, it is difficult to view this play through the same eyes as an Elizabethan audience. Shylock has reason for demanding his revenge against Antonio and the Christians and it is not hard to feel sympathy for his total humiliation at the hands of his disloyal daughter. He is totally subjugated at the end of the play, and has everything stripped away from him, even his religion.

THINK ABOUT IT

Jews were a despised race to Elizabethans. One of the few trades open to them was usury, or money lending for interest; a trade banned to Christians. They lived in segregation, and were in fact 'ghettoised'.

In the light of the events of the Second World War, how do we feel about this kind of racism now?

N
O
T
E
S

Antonio is the main character; the events are shaped around his money. It is his financial loss and then gain which dictates the pace of the dramatic action. He loses his fortune temporarily so that Shylock can appear to be in a position of strength. He narrowly escapes death by a clever twist of legal wordplay from Portia. His wealth is then restored, more glorious than imagined. Thus the play ends with all the worthwhile characters appearing to get what they want.

The love plot is also closely linked to the idea of money and financial gain. Portia is a prize to be won – 'a lady richly left'. Bassanio wins her in the casket game, giving her the status of object rather than independent woman. Her powerful, intelligent language show her to be far more than this, however. She wins Antonio's life when all others are powerless to help, although she has to dress as a man and enter the 'male' world in order to do this.

The court scene of Act IV is the high point of dramatic tension. The events of Act V can appear frivolous alongside the thunderous drama preceding them. However, Shakespeare needed Act V to consolidate the good fortune of all the remaining characters. He also gives us the ring plot here. This has a comic function on one level, but closely links to the rest of the play by confirming the two sets of lovers as right for each other. Both Bassanio and Gratiano have to earn their wives rather than simply win them. Both men learn what prizes they have 'won' and that they should treasure them. The events of Act V therefore give a satisfactory conclusion for the audience.

First performances for the Court of James I, around 1604

Macbeth, an officer and soldier for King Duncan of Scotland, is prophesied by witches to become King. His own ambition and the pressing of his fiercely ambitious wife leads him to kill his King in order to become ruler of Scotland. His brief period of power is fraught with guilt and paranoia, and he is eventually conquered and executed by an army led by the rightful heir to the throne.

Plot

This is a violent story of the tragic consequences of greed, violence and ambition. Macbeth is a Scottish soldier and nobleman, brave and fierce. He is highly thought of by his peers and the king. King Duncan rewards him for his bravery in the war against Norway. However, Macbeth is also very ambitious. Immediately after the victory against Norway, he is met by three witches who already know of Macbeth's fatal flaw and taunt him with the hope of greatness by telling him that he will become, firstly, Thane of Cawdor and then king.

When the first of these prophesies comes true almost immediately after this meeting, Macbeth begins to take the first steps towards his own eventual downfall by telling his ambitious wife of the prophesy. Lady Macbeth leaps on this news, and the pair are further goaded into action when King

Duncan decides to visit them at their castle, thus giving them the perfect opportunity to kill him.

After Macbeth is crowned king, he becomes obsessed with the idea of peace of mind. He convinces himself that he will only be at peace when he has eradicated all those who suspect him of the murder, when in fact it is his own guilty conscience which torments him. He has his best friend Banquo killed, followed by the wife and family of Macduff, another nobleman who refuses to bow to Macbeth as king.

He pays another visit to the witches, who play with his mind by giving him more riddling prophesies which he interprets as promises that he is invincible. However, his life becomes more and more empty and unhappy as he loses all his friends and becomes a cold-blooded monster. His wife's suicide is the last straw for him when he finally realises that his life is worthless and meaningless. There is a sense of relief when Macduff arrives with an English army to unseat him from the throne. He is killed by Macduff and the Scottish crown is given to Duncan's son Malcolm.

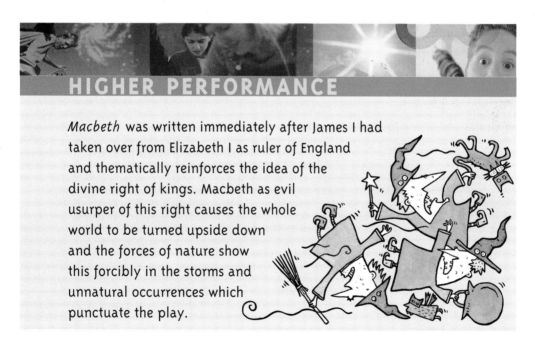

HIGHER PERFORMANCE

Macbeth was written immediately after James I had taken over from Elizabeth I as ruler of England and thematically reinforces the idea of the divine right of kings. Macbeth as evil usurper of this right causes the whole world to be turned upside down and the forces of nature show this forcibly in the storms and unnatural occurrences which punctuate the play.

Main Themes

Ambition

The character of Macbeth embodies the theme of ambition. At the start of the play he is already in a powerful position but has clearly already entertained ideas of being greater, otherwise why would the witches bother attempting to manipulate him?

Macbeth is not patient in his ambition; his tragedy is that he does not wait for the 'greatness' but takes terrible steps to achieve too much too quickly.

Macbeth's ambition is his 'fatal flaw' and the driving force of the play. The tragedy is that he chooses to listen to his wife and the witches rather than his conscience. His ambition is too strong to resist temptation, in spite of the knowledge that he has no justification for his actions.

Duty and responsibility

Everyone has his place in the hierarchy of this world; Duncan as ruler, his sons next to him in power and authority, his officers Banquo, Macduff, Macbeth, Lennox and Ross next, and so on. Each position carries with it its share of responsibility and these appear to be very clear to all. When Macbeth commits his murderous deed, all rules are reversed.

DID YOU KNOW?
Macbeth would have been intimately related to the Gunpowder Plot in 1605 and the scale of that treachery made the events of the play seem topical indeed.

Evil and the supernatural

The witches direct this play. They open it with their plotting and set the scene for evil and supernatural events. They know that Macbeth is corruptible and feed his ambition with their half-truths.

Macbeth is full of supernatural occurrences such as the dagger which directs Macbeth, and Banquo's ghost which taunts him at the banquet.

Structure

Exposition

The witches appear first, setting the scene of evil and the supernatural. They are quickly followed by the soldier, hurrying to give Duncan news of Macbeth's bravery in battle and thus showing him to be in an honoured position at the start of the play.

Development

The witches greet Macbeth and his 'rapt' reaction to their words shows the future course of events. Duncan's plan to stay at Macbeth's castle gives him opportunity. His wife takes over the plotting.

Crisis

The murder of Duncan takes place. Macbeth is crowned king of Scotland.

N
O
T
E
S

Redevelopment

Macbeth commits further atrocities and turns everyone against him by his actions as king. Macduff, Malcolm and others join forces with the English to overthrow him. Lady Macbeth commits suicide, tormented by guilt.

Catastrophe

When Macduff explains the riddle of the witches' words, Macbeth learns that he has been conned. His final valiant stand, 'then lay on, Macduff!', is without intensity and has the inevitability of failure.

Denouement

Malcolm takes the throne of Scotland.

Macbeth is a tragedy, therefore the structure follows a clear and distinct pattern. The tragic hero has to have an elevated status at the start of the play, from which he plummets towards his downfall.

The witches introduce the play, setting the tone for evil and supernatural events. Violence quickly follows, with a description of Macbeth's bravery in his loyal fighting for Scotland in the battle against Norway. When Macbeth enters with a line which echoes the speech of the witches from two scenes before, 'So foul and fair a day I have not seen', he is instantly linked with the witches in the minds of the audience.

Macbeth's lofty status is compounded by being awarded the title Thane of Cawdor. His place in Duncan's trust is assured. However, Duncan's description of the traitorous Cawdor should also pose as a warning bell – 'He was a gentleman on whom I built an absolute trust'. The traitor and Macbeth are now linked by the same title.

Closing Thoughts

The action moves swiftly towards Duncan's murder as Macbeth and his wife are given opportunity to act out their plan. The plotting is brief; Lady Macbeth wastes no time in coming up with a plan of military precision, which clearly appeals to the soldier in her husband. The murder is carried out in darkness, in a state of acute tension. Once committed, the central characters leave the stage to the Porter, who changes the focus momentarily with his ironic, comic speech about 'devil-portering'.

Macbeth's time as king is probably intended to last for some months; long enough for him to establish himself as a despotic ruler, careless of his country and its people. However, this is impossible to show on stage; thus the information is related through the commentaries of other characters. His descent into paranoia and madness remains the focus; the murder of Banquo, the second visit to the witches, the savage and brutal attack on Macduff's castle are the dramatic events which are staged to show how far Macbeth has fallen from his lofty position.

By the time Macduff arrives to challenge Macbeth and avenge the death of his family, Macbeth and the audience are aware that his defeat is assured. He has nothing left to fight for, and the suicide of Lady Macbeth immediately prior to Macduff's entrance only marks this more clearly. Macbeth comments that life is a waste of time, pointless and without purpose – 'Life's but a walking shadow; a poor player'.
His death is necessary for the tragedy to have an end; it is the only satisfactory conclusion to events. He could not possibly live on after all that he has done.

One of the last plays, probably dated around 1611

Prospero, the usurped duke of Milan, is abandoned on an uninhabited island with his daughter Miranda. He practises his magical powers and waits for the time when he can enact revenge upon his disloyal brother and regain control of his kingdom.

Plot

Generally thought of as Shakespeare's last play, this is the one which has caused most controversy of interpretation. It is a play full of magic, dominated by Prospero the magician, the rightful Duke of Milan, who has been usurped by his brother Antonio and cast away onto a desert island with his daughter Miranda. Prospero takes over the island and enslaves the previous human inhabitant Caliban, the son of Sycorax the witch. He attempts to civilise Caliban the savage, teaching him language and the ways of the world. However Caliban cannot totally overcome his natural savagery and attempts to rape Miranda. He remains defiant of Prospero's rule – 'you have taught me language, and my profit on't is; I know how to curse'.

Prospero's magic tells him that a ship containing his brother, together with the King of Naples, his son Ferdinand and other noblemen is drawing near the island. Prospero conjures up a storm to have them shipwrecked. Ferdinand and

Miranda meet and fall in love. Caliban meets two unreliable servants and the three decide to rebel against their masters and escape. All of this is watched and manipulated by Prospero, who secretes Ferdinand and Miranda away so that the others believe them lost.

Prospero eventually explains everything to the astonished castaways; Alonso is overjoyed to have his son (Ferdinand) returned to him and staggered at the news that it is in fact Prospero and not Antonio who is the rightful Duke of Milan. Prospero feels he can finally rest now that he has been vindicated and that he can return to his dukedom. The wrongdoers can be punished and Prospero is delighted that his daughter will have made a match with the inherent Duke of Naples.

HIGHER PERFORMANCE

The Tempest is a play about control and domination. Many assert that, as Shakespeare's final work, it was indeed a comment on his career of controlling the stage life of his characters, and was in itself a valedictory comment on his life's work.

How far would you agree with that assertion and why?

Main Themes

Nature versus nurture

Prospero attempts to educate or 'nurture' Caliban, but it backfires when Caliban uses the tool of language against his master. The question of whether Caliban would have been better off without Prospero's interference runs through the play. 'Does education change us?' is the question being addressed.

The nature of love

The love between parent and child is a strong theme, as is that between master and servant, man for his country and the purity of romantic love between man and woman.

Magic

In Shakespeare's time, most people believed in the power of the supernatural. This was largely because the world seemed to be a place where there were no explanations for much of what happened. Science was a limited study and people needed a way of explaining the world. Thus superstition and magic were real beliefs, as was the absolute belief in God. This play is dominated by magic like no other of Shakespeare's plays. The characters seldom act of their own free will; all events are controlled, 'staged' by Prospero and his 'art'.

Some say that this play was a metaphor for Shakespeare himself; he controlled the action on the stage in the same way that Prospero controlled the action on the island.

Usurpation and colonialism

Prospero takes over and colonises the deserted island, just as the English were colonising most of the world. Does he have a right to that much authority? Shakespeare is highlighting contemporary moral concerns about the activities of the colonists. There are also echoes to the activities of the

monarchies in Shakespeare's recent history. Caliban, Stephano and Trinculo all attempt to overthrow their masters, all unsuccessfully. Ariel is only freed from his bondage when Prospero has no further use for him.

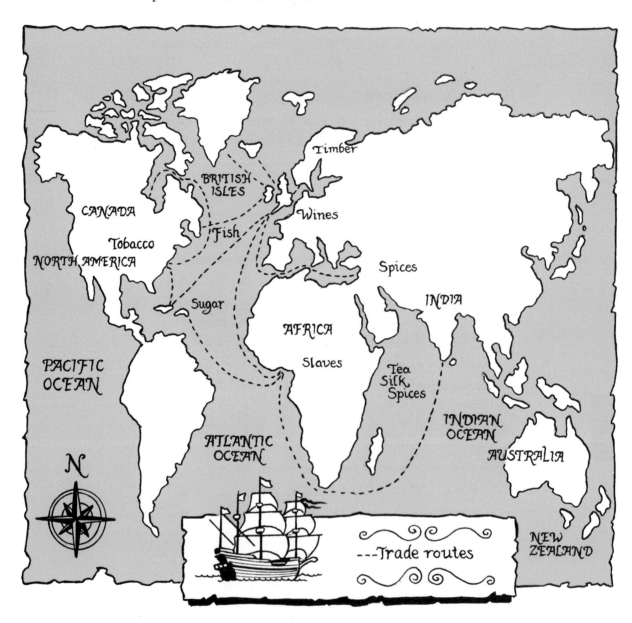

Structure

Exposition

The play opens with a shipwreck, setting the scene and giving a strong thematic message of the power of elemental forces. Prospero explains to Miranda her history and his own betrayal at the hands of his brother.

Development

Caliban attempts his rape of Miranda and makes his rebellious feelings known to Prospero. Miranda sees Ferdinand and falls in love with him.

Crisis

Caliban attempts to overthrow Prospero and enlists the help of Stephano and Trinculo in doing so.

Redevelopment

Caliban's attempts are halted by Prospero. Miranda and Ferdinand are promised to each other.

Catastrophe

Prospero reveals his true identity to the shipwrecked visitors. The marriage is sealed. Ariel is freed. Caliban is punished.

Denouement

Prospero delivers his valedictory speech to the audience.

Remember the dramatic unities? ⊙ **see pp 17-18** Shakespeare stuck closely to the unity of time in *The Tempest*. The action takes place over a period of four hours, during which an awful lot happens! We have to take a step back from the real world in order to accept that the events do occur in such a short time; in

N O T E S

other words, 'suspend our belief' and immerse ourselves in the world of the play.

In order to create a fully-rounded story in such a short span of time, we are given a good deal of important information by the use of narration. In Act I Scene 2, Prospero tells his daughter Miranda the story of her birth and the events that led up to them being cast away from their home and onto the island. The main plot concerns the story of Prospero's betrayal at the hands of his brother, which he revenges by the use of his 'art', magic. This ties in neatly to the love story between Miranda and Ferdinand. Their love cements the ties between Milan and Naples, and gives Prospero an ally with which to defeat his scheming brother.

The subplot of Caliban, Stephano and Trinculo echoes the main plot of usurpation of power by treachery. This minor rebellion against Prospero's authority is doomed to failure because these characters are subordinate in intelligence as well as power. The strong message is that wrong can never be successful for long, and that any gain by treachery is short-lived. The fumbled attempts of these three are soon uncovered and punished.

Closing Thoughts

In *The Tempest*, Shakespeare raises many issues that would have been interesting to his audience of the time. The Elizabethan and Jacobean periods were a time of great religious upheaval and his themes would have been relevant and topical. He explores sin, repentance, forgiveness and magic – all in the timespan of four short hours!

Shakespeare also examines the relationship between sophisticated, educated man and unsophisticated man. However, none of the characters fall neatly into either category; Caliban embodies 'The Noble Savage', capable of acts of barbarity, such as the attempted rape of Miranda, yet at the same time he has a love of music and nature. Prospero, a philosopher in the true sense of the word shows himself to be educated and cultured, but he seeks to colonise Caliban's island for himself, and presumes to educate him to his standards and beliefs. He dismisses Ariel when he has outlived his usefulness. Who can say whose beliefs are right and whose are wrong? Who is really the most appealing character? This is why *The Tempest* is one of Shakespeare's most challenging plays.

DID YOU KNOW?
Our word philosophy comes from joining two Greek words, **philos** and **sophos**, meaning love and wisdom. You'll come across these two Greek words a lot as you study; an oeno**phile** is a connoisseur, or lover of wine, and a **soph**omore is an American secondary school student who is, we hope, gaining wisdom!

The Tempest is an optimistic play, the language less image-laden than many of Shakespeare's other works, with words such as 'beauty', 'noble', 'virtue' and 'nature' repeated often. As Shakespeare's final play, its complexity and ideas are a fitting tribute to a playwright whose works embody universal truths.

HIGHER PERFORMANCE

1 Discuss how the theme of financial risk is shown in *The Merchant of Venice*.

2 Compare and contrast the changing power status between Macbeth and his wife before and after the pivotal murder of Duncan.

3 Describe the difficulties faced by William Shakespeare in the portrayal of strong female characters and show how he overcame these difficulties with particular reference to one female character.

4 Is Prospero a kindly magician or a power-crazed sorcerer?

5 Choose a good film version of a Shakespeare text and watch it; most libraries have video copies of nearly every available film/television version of the plays. Write yourself some notes on what you observed from the experience of watching the performance as opposed to a dry reading of the text.

Quiz

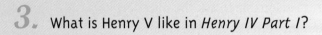

1. Who are the two people who help Romeo and Juliet?

2. Why do the Montagues and Capulets hate each other?

3. What is Henry V like in *Henry IV Part I*?

4. At which two places does Henry V make stirring speeches to his men?

5. Who provides comedy in *Henry V*?

6. What is the alternative title of *Twelfth Night*?

7. What is the name of Shylock's daughter?

8. Which religion is Shylock forced to adopt?

9. Who kills Macbeth?

10. Who is Caliban's mother?

Answers

1. The Nurse and Friar Lawrence.
2. We don't really know!
3. Wild and reckless.
4. Harfleur and Agincourt.
5. Captain Fluellen.
6. *What You Will.*
7. Jessica.
8. Christianity.
9. Macduff.
10. Sycorax the witch.

SHAKESPEARE'S RELEVANCE TODAY

Art imitating life
Relevance to English study
William Shakespeare the Elizabethan

Art imitating life

As a student of Shakespeare, it is reasonable to ask the question 'why all this fuss about a playwright who has been dead for nearly four hundred years? What can his plays possibly have to do with my world today?'

This is very good question and one which anyone who takes the study of Shakespeare seriously will ask themselves many times.

- Shakespeare remains fascinating because the themes of his plays have relevance to our world

- He writes about human nature, which surprisingly hasn't changed much over the years

- Strong emotions like passion, jealousy and anger are not inventions of the twentieth century!

- He writes about the relationship between parents and children, of passionate love, of sex, violence, greed and betrayal, and makes the stories so relevant that they still have loads to offer today

THINK ABOUT IT

Art imitating life – Shakespeare's themes are interesting, that is why he wrote about them. It is also may be significant that most modern soap-operas concentrate on exactly the same things – love, hate, jealousy, revenge, power ... because that is what most average humans are interested in. William Shakespeare was no fool, it seems!

Relevance to English study

The National Curriculum states that every student should have access to at least two complete plays by William Shakespeare during Key Stages 3 and 4.

By studying Shakespeare, we develop skills highlighted in the National Curriculum:

- Analysing character and plot
- The use of imagery
- Selecting and sifting information
- Appreciation of techniques
- Reflecting on a writer's presentation of ideas
- The motivation and behaviour of characters
- Appreciating the overall impact of a text
- Appreciation of the characteristics that distinguish literature of high quality

The theatre

The masses could not generally read, and did not have televisions and cinemas. But they wanted entertainment and the theatre provided this. Groups of 'strolling' players, or itinerant theatre companies, sprang up everywhere and were in great demand. Theatres sprang up all over London; The Theatre, opened in 1576, was the first purpose-built theatre for plays. It was closely followed by The Curtain in 1577. The most famous theatre, The Globe, was home to William Shakespeare and his company.

In order to run a theatre company, you needed a patron – someone with the money and power to give you backing in your endeavours. Shakespeare's patron was the Lord Chamberlain under Elizabeth I's reign: The Globe Theatre became the home of The Lord Chamberlain's Men and Shakespeare was writer for this company. The Globe could hold around three thousand people, who all paid either a penny or two pence depending on whether they wanted to stand in 'the belly' of the stalls or get a seat in one of the many galleries going around the stage. Everything was very informal and extremely basic. It was set up in 1599 and had fourteen years of frenzied activity before it burned to the ground in 1613.

Of course all of the plays were performed there, but there were also other, 'private' showings at court. In 1603, James I came to the English throne, and he took over patronage of The Lord Chamberlain's Men – who became The King's Men.

THE GLOBE THEATRE,

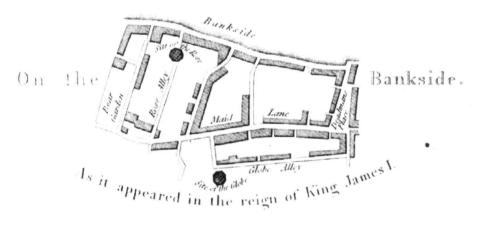

On the Bankside.

As it appeared in the reign of King James I.

William Shakespeare the Elizabethan

Every writer is a product of his own time. Shakespeare was born in Stratford-upon-Avon in 1564 and began writing at a time of immense change and artistic productivity – the like of which has never been repeated in history. The Renaissance dramatically focussed attention on artistic endeavours. Furthermore, the arts became for the first time a product for the masses, not just the courtly elite. His own productivity echoes the rapid movement of the times.

Historical context

This was a living, breathing world of political intrigue, huge unrest and instability. Elizabeth I was the first ever Protestant ruler of England. Her father, Henry VIII, had created a Protestant church and made himself and his descendants head. This was due to an argument with the Pope and Henry's subsequent excommunication. All through Elizabeth's reign, she had been plagued by threats of a Catholic takeover; the most powerful of which was from her half-sister Mary, Queen of Scots, who the Catholics said was the rightful ruler of England. Mary had some very powerful supporters; not least of which were the rulers of Spain and France – both Catholic nations. It was only with the defeat of the Spanish Armada that England looked set to have a period of political and religious stability.

A recurrent theme in Shakespeare's plays is the nature of rulership; stressing the value of constitutional change rather than revolution. The Elizabethan times were very turbulent and the plays echo this, while at the same time reinforcing the stability of the crown itself. Shakespeare was a realist, a pragmatist; he was also a man of the world he inhabited.

When James I came to the throne in 1603, William Shakespeare had to re-align himself to a Catholic monarch. He obviously succeeded well! *Macbeth* was written for James I and performed at court before it ever reached The Globe. *Macbeth* is all about the divine right of kingship and the ultimate fall of those who oppose this divine right. Shakespeare was no fool; he was a diplomat who had to work hard to maintain his place at court and in the public eye.

Shakespeare was not writing in a vacuum. He can only be understood against the background of his own time. For instance, when we consider how women are represented in the plays, we have to remember that women held a far less equal status in society than they do today.

Similarly our attitudes towards other cultures have altered rapidly. No one can study *The Merchant of Venice* without having to think carefully about the circumstances and attitudes which surrounded Shakespeare when he was writing. He did not know about The Holocaust. In his day, Jews were roundly despised and seen as a race apart. It is really hard to try and think about the subject of a play written four hundred years ago with a twentieth-century set of assumptions, but it is the only way really to understand the intention of the play.

We can be really grateful that Shakespeare was such a man of his time, because the thirty-seven plays certainly give an extraordinary amount of information about how people thought, felt and behaved in sixteenth-century England.

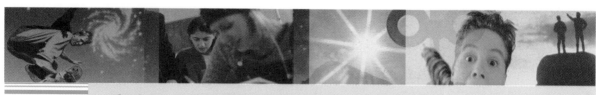

Shakespeare's life

1. When and where was William Shakespeare born?

2. How many plays did he write altogether?

3. Who became Queen in 1558?

4. What is the meaning of the term 'Renaissance'?

5. What is the name of the theatre in London where most of the plays were first seen?

6. In what year was this theatre destroyed by fire?

7. What was the name of William Shakespeare's theatre company, taken from the name of the person who patronised them?

8. How old was William Shakespeare when he died?

9. Where did William Shakespeare get the ideas for his plays?

Answers

1. Stratford-upon-Avon, 1564.
2. 37.
3. Elizabeth.
4. Rebirth.
5. The Globe.
6. 1613.
7. The Lord Chamberlain's Men, later The King's Men, after James I who patronised them.
8. 52.
9. History books, old French and Italian romance tales.

Did you get it?

Theatrical conventions

1. Who was the great thinker whose ideas on theatre conventions formed the basis for most modern drama?

2. What happy event nearly always happens at the end of a Shakespearean comedy?

3. Why is there a category sometimes referred to as 'the problem plays'?

4. Why did William Shakespeare create more male roles than female ones?

5. Which ancient civilisation gives us the foundations for most of our theatrical conventions?

6. How did Elizabethan playwrights deal with the limited props, scenery, costume and effects available to them?

7. What was the dramatic function of the Chorus?

8. How many syllables are in one line of blank verse?

9. What is the difference between blank verse and prose?

10. What is meant by the term 'fatal flaw' and which type of character has one?

Answers

1. Aristotle.
2. Marriage.
3. They have elements of tragedy and comedy and are difficult to put clearly into one category.
4. Women were not allowed to act.
5. Greece.
6. Language created atmosphere and setting.
7. To add background information, about events not depicted on stage.
8. 10.
9. Verse has rhythm and recognisable metre.
10. A negative character trait which leads to eventual downfall, always held by tragic hero.

Key plays

1. What does Macbeth do to become king of Scotland?

2. Who is Miranda's father?

3. Who kills Mercutio?

4. How does Bassanio win the hand of Portia?

5. What does Shylock demand of Antonio?

6. In which play do three witches appear?

7. What does the French Dauphin send to *Henry V* as an insulting message?

8. Who is the villainous character of *Twelfth Night*, his name taken from a word meaning 'evil'?

9. Who eventually kills Macbeth?

10. 'Cesario' is really who in *Twelfth Night*?

Answers

1. Kills his king, King Duncan.
2. Prospero.
3. Tybalt – in a play-fight which Romeo tries to stop.
4. By correctly answering the casket riddle set by her father.
5. One pound of Antonio's flesh.
6. *Macbeth*.
7. A box of tennis balls.
8. Malvolio.
9. Macduff.
10. Viola.

Did you get it?

Essay practice

Here are a few questions that require you to write a more lengthy response to a question on William Shakespeare. You be the judge of how much you should write, but make sure you have answered the question fully and brought in some evidence in the form of textual reference wherever possible and relevant. Discuss your answers with your friends and teachers.

1. Who is most to blame for the deaths of Mercutio and Tybalt in *Romeo and Juliet*?

2. Is Macbeth solely responsible for the events of the play, or are there other elements partially to blame?

3. What is a theme, and how is it different from a plot? Illustrate your answer with reference to one play.

4. Imagine you are a big Hollywood producer. Choose one of the plays and cast it from any famous actors you choose. Give reasons for your choices.

5. The recent film version of *Romeo and Juliet* is set in a large, violent American city. Taking any of the other plays, decide where you would set it and describe the reasons why. You need to refer to the play in your answer.

Index